W9-CCN-495

YOU CAN
—WITH—
BEAKMAN
Science Stuff
You Can Do
by JOK CHURCH

Andrews and McMeel
A Universal Press Syndicate Company
Kansas City

You Can with Beakman is distributed by Universal Press Syndicate.

You Can with Beakman: Science Stuff You Can Do copyright © 1992 by Universal Press Syndicate. All rights reserved. Printed in the United States of America. No part of this book may be used or reproduced in any manner whatsoever without written permission except in the context of reviews. For information, write Andrews and McMeel, a Universal Press Syndicate Company, 4900 Main Street, Kansas City, Missouri 64112.

Printed on recycled paper.

Library of Congress Cataloging-in-Publication Data:

Church, Jok.
    You can with Beakman : science stuff you can do/by Jok Church.
        p.   cm.
    Summary: A collection of science experiments exploring such topics as apples, blood, and feet smell.
    ISBN 0-8362-7004-5 (pbk.): $8.95
        1. Science—Experiments—Juvenile literature. [1. Science--Experiments.
        2. Experiments.]
    Q164.C447   1992
    507.8—dc20
                                                            92-24979
                                                            CIP
                                                            AC

NOTE TO PARENTS:
You Can with Beakman: Science Stuff You Can Do is intended to be educational and informative. It contains relatively simple science experiments designed to interest children. Many of the experiments require adult supervision. We strongly recommend that before you allow children to conduct any of the experiments in this book that you read the experiment in its entirety and make your own determination as to the safest way of conducting the experiment.

ATTENTION: SCHOOLS AND BUSINESSES
Andrews and McMeel books are available at quantity discounts with bulk purchase for educational, business, or sales promotional use. For information, write to Special Sales Department, Andrews and McMeel, 4900 Main Street, Kansas City, Missouri 64112.

CONTENTS

Stuff You Can Do to Figure Out . . .

ACKNOWLEDGMENTS

You Can with Beakman is the first comic strip ever to be written, drawn and color separated entirely on a computer—a Macintosh IIci. Turning a bunch of my computer files into this electronically published book was a monumental task—impossible without the creativity, talents, gifts and patience of the Andrews and McMeel and Universal Press Syndicate staff members listed here:

Julie Phillips—page layout design and computer graphics goddess; Dorothy O'Brien—got this thing published and made sure the grammar was done good; Tammy Shanahan—guided this through the twists and turns of deadline mania; Susan Patton—waded through my confusing computer files; Carlos Corredor—made sure the color separations sparkled; Traci Bertz—worked with the printer to make sure this could really be done.

All have my deepest appreciation and highest regard.

I would also like to acknowledge the people who had faith in me, even in the toughest of times:

Marsha Fine and Glenn Peck—on vibes; Von Wall—kept me employed and made me laugh; Deborah Gump—published my comic strip before everyone else; Lisa Tarry—every week: helps (me) find new ways - to punctuate; Lee Salem—picked my comic out of the hundreds he could have chosen; Barb Thompson—made sure Lee took my calls; Bev Shiels and Rita Denton—Keepers of the High Gate and secrets therein; Florence Mills—Mom who loves me and weeps at moments like this; Charlie Church—crazy artist father who put paintbrushes in a 7-year-old's hand and told him to go create something pretty on the garage door.

A portion of royalties are donated to the Marin Community Food Bank because they feed kids and because we don't hear much about the 1,000 points of light anymore.

To my newspaper readers:
"Thank you for teaching me everything I know."

For Adam Ciesielski, who shares life

Dear Reader:

⚠️ Please look for this special caution sign throughout this book. When you see this sign, it means that you need to ask a grown-up for help.

This is a book for families to use together so the grown-ups in your family should be happy to work with you.

Show your family this page. Remember, look for this sign. It is very important. ⚠️

Beakman

Beakman

Dear Beakman,

Why do pictures look so much better in my View-Master?

Janet

Dear Janet,

Most pictures are just tall and wide. Pictures in your View-Master are tall, wide and deep. Depth is the 3rd Dimension. That's where the word 3-D comes from. Here are two experiments *You Can* do to learn how 3-D works.

Beakman

Beakman

Seeing the Two Different Pictures

WHAT YOU NEED: Just a pencil

WHAT TO DO: Hold the pencil about 18 inches from your face and look at a window on the other side of the room. Focus on the pencil and notice the window. Now focus on the window and notice the pencil.

WHAT IS GOING ON:

When you looked at the pencil you saw 2 windows behind it. When you looked at the window you saw 2 pencils in front of it. There is really only 1 pencil and 1 window. What you are really seeing is 2 different pictures; 1 for each eye. Try the experiment again with only 1 eye open. You'll see just 1 window and 1 pencil. People who have only 1 eye that works cannot see depth. They cannot see in 3-D.

This Book Is Getting Deep

WHAT YOU NEED: This book

WHAT TO DO: Hold the book about 12 inches from your face and look at the trees on the next page. Now cross your eyes so you can see 3 images instead of 2. Pay attention to the picture in the middle. The trick is to focus your eyes while they are crossed. It may take some time. *You Can* do it. Relax and be patient.

WHAT IS GOING ON:

You Can see the tree nearest you and the one that is far away. The two pictures are not the same. When your brain puts them together, you get 3-D. Do not look too long. Crossing your eyes can give you a headache.

The World Is Already in 3-D

We use the 3rd dimension — depth — to tell how far away things are. Humans and other animals need to do that, which is why we have 2 eyes. Each eye sees a slightly different picture.

When our brain puts those two pictures together, we get a 3-D image.

Your View-Master does the same thing. Each eye piece shows you a slightly different picture. Your brain puts them together and you see in 3-D.

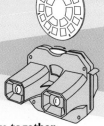

Each eye sees its own picture. The brain puts them together.

9

Dear Beakman,

Do airplanes fly because they go so fast? My brother runs with his arms out. He thinks he will fly.

Bill

Dear Bill,

It isn't just speed that lifts a heavy airplane up in the sky. It is something called air pressure. *You Can* do these experiments to see how air pressure can push a big jet up into the sky.

Beakman

WHAT YOU NEED: A clean plastic bottle. Your lungs.

WHAT TO DO: Look at the sides of the bottle. Then, with your mouth suck some of the air out of the bottle. What happened? Why do you think it happened?

WHAT IS GOING ON:
When you took air out of the bottle you lowered the air pressure inside it. The air pressure outside the bottle is greater, so it pushed the sides of the bottle in. Any time air pressure is not the same, the higher air pressure will push toward the lower air pressure. It is trying to make the air pressure balanced, or the same. It is the air OUTSIDE of the bottle that pushed in the sides!

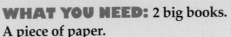

WHAT YOU NEED: 2 big books. A piece of paper.

WHAT TO DO: Put the big books four inches apart and lay the paper on top. Stoop down so you are even with the table and try blowing UNDER the paper to lift the paper up. Blow hard! What happened?

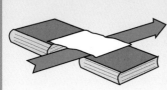

WHAT IS GOING ON:
When you blew under the paper you lowered the air pressure in the little space between the books. The higher air pressure on top of the paper pushed it down - not up like we think it would.

WHAT YOU NEED: A piece of paper - tape - scissors - pencil - canister vacuum cleaner (a kind of vacuum)

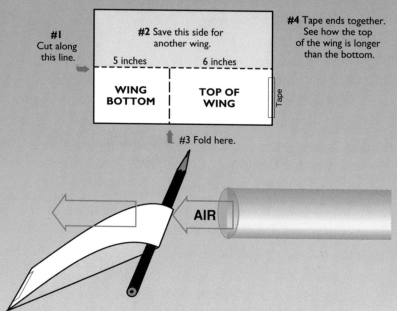

#1 Cut along this line.

#2 Save this side for another wing.

5 inches | 6 inches

WING BOTTOM | **TOP OF WING**

Tape

#4 Tape ends together. See how the top of the wing is longer than the bottom.

#3 Fold here.

AIR

WHAT TO DO: Look at the drawing and make a wing. Hold it with the pencil against the back of your vacuum cleaner - the end where the air blows out. Move it up until the air is blowing over the TOP of your wing. What happened?

WHAT IS GOING ON:
When you blew air over the top of the wing, you lowered the air pressure. The air pressure on the bottom of the wing is greater, so it pushed the wing UP. Air pressure pushing up from the bottom of the wing is what keeps airplanes up in the air.

Dear Beakman,

Why does an apple turn brown after you bite into it?

Jamie

Dear Jamie,

Your apple is turning brown because another chemical is mixing with it. The chemical is oxygen – the same stuff we need to live. Lots of foods turn brown. But there are ways of slowing that process down. The chemicals that slow down browning have to be listed on the labels of food you buy at the grocery store. The next time you go shopping, read the labels. There's tons of information on labels. To keep your apples from turning brown, add another fruit, or add a vitamin C tablet. Really.

Beakman

Beakman

Kitchen Chemistry

WHAT YOU NEED: One or more of these fruits: apples - pears - peaches - bananas - lemon. *OPTIONAL: Vitamin C tablets - vinegar*

WHAT TO DO: Peel and slice up all the fruit except the lemon. You should have a grown-up help you if this is new to you. Divide the fruit into 2 bowls. Leave one bowl alone. Squeeze the lemon into the other and toss the fruit until it's all covered with the lemon juice.

OPTIONAL: Crush the vitamin C tablet in between 2 spoons. Dissolve it in 3/4 cup water. Use that instead of lemon juice. Or use a teaspoon of vinegar in a quart of water.

WHAT IS GOING ON: All of the fruits you sliced up will turn brown if allowed to mix with oxygen in the air. The lemon juice, vitamin C and vinegar are all weak acids that slow down that process. They are called antioxidants (ant-i-AHK-sed-untz). The fruit you didn't add anything to will turn brown in several hours. When we experiment, that is called the *control group*. We can compare it to the *experimental group* – which is the fruit you changed with the weak acids. They won't turn brown as fast. In fact, if you add a little yogurt and a bit of honey, you have a fruit salad!

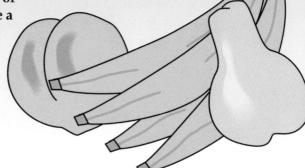

Turning Apples Brown on Purpose

WHAT YOU NEED: Apple - 3% peroxide from the medicine chest - food processor/blender - help and permission from a grown-up in your family.

WHAT TO DO: Cut up an apple and put it in the food processor. Add 1/4 cup peroxide. Have the grown-up blend them together till it's moosh. Pour it out into a clear bowl or cup and wait 30 minutes. It'll be very brown. *You Can* even watch it happen.

⚠ *CAUTION:* DO NOT DRINK this liquid. It's not good for you and you could get sick. Throw it away.

WHAT IS GOING ON: Inside the little cells in the apple are all kinds of chemicals. Some of them are called aldehydes (AL-duh-hides). One of them is called 5-hydroxymethylfurfural, which is a real mouthful. When oxygen mixes with these chemicals, they turn brown. Peroxide releases oxygen. The blender cut open the cells and released the aldehydes. Together they turn a yucky brown. When this browning happens in the air – and not in an experiment – the fruit is perfectly safe and good to eat. Your experiment is NOT safe to eat. Again, throw it away.

Dear Readers,

Arbor Day is a special day set aside to plant trees. It's celebrated the last Friday of April. Here's some help.

Beakman

Dear Readers,

Arbor Day is a great time to dig a hole and plant a tree. "Arbor" is a word in Latin—a very old language. It means tree. I planted trees on Arbor Day when I was 10 years old. Today, the trees I planted are big and give me a lot of pleasure and joy. I hope *You Can* have that same joy yourself.

Also, planting a tree is fun and a good thing to do for the planet.

Beakman

Beakman

How to Plant a Tree

1 Take charge. Ask your family if it's OK to plant a tree. Tell them about Arbor Day. Promise to make the project your responsibility. Get people excited about it.

2 Figure out where the tree should be planted. Make sure it won't get in the way of other trees or things like power lines and pipes.

3 Find a plant nursery by looking in the Yellow Pages.

4 Go there with your family and talk to the people who work there. Ask them to suggest the kind of tree you'll plant. Buy a baby tree, called a sapling (SAP-ling). They are inexpensive.

5 Make sure the people at the nursery explain details on planting the tree. Take a pad and pencil and take notes.

6 Use the notes when you plant the tree.

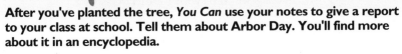

After you've planted the tree, *You Can* use your notes to give a report to your class at school. Tell them about Arbor Day. You'll find more about it in an encyclopedia.

Why It's Good for the Planet

Trees and people have one thing in common—glucose (GLOO-cos), a very simple sugar. We use it as a food. When we make glucose, we use oxygen. One thing that's left over is carbon dioxide.

Trees make glucose in a different way. They use carbon dioxide, and the thing that's left over is oxygen.

We need the thing trees don't need (oxygen) and trees need the thing we don't (carbon dioxide). It's one of those Nature-in-balance things. The trick is making sure there are enough trees around.

If planting a tree at home is impossible, don't give up. Suggest it to your class as something you can all do together. That way *You Can* share the work and the responsibility of making sure your tree gets water.

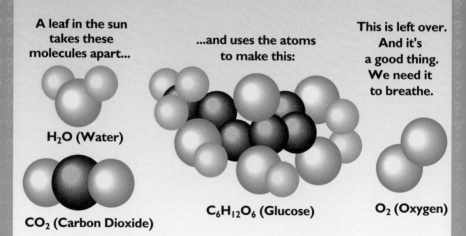

A leaf in the sun takes these molecules apart...

...and uses the atoms to make this:

This is left over. And it's a good thing. We need it to breathe.

H_2O (Water)

CO_2 (Carbon Dioxide)

$C_6H_{12}O_6$ (Glucose)

O_2 (Oxygen)

The little numbers tell you how many atoms there are in that molecule. Water is H_2O, or 2 hydrogen atoms with 1 atom of oxygen.

Dear Beakman,

Why is blood so important?

Renée

Dear Renée,

Blood does lots of work in our bodies. And all of it is important. If just one of the jobs that blood does isn't done, we're in big trouble. Blood is better when it's inside, so this experiment doesn't involve bleeding. You'll have to use your memory to think back to the last time you really saw blood.

Beakman

Beakman

Lots of Different Jobs
All of them important

Here is a list of some of the things blood does. Our bodies need all of these jobs done.

1 SUPPLIES oxygen to every living cell
2 REMOVES carbon dioxide from every living cell
3 FEEDS nutrients to every cell
4 REMOVES waste from the cells
5 HELPS regulate our body's temperature
6 FIGHTS infection and disease

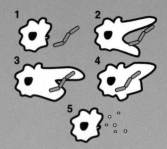

Our blood attacks diseases with its white blood cells. A white blood cell attacks a bacterium (germ) by surrounding it, breaking it into pieces and sometimes spitting out what's left.

Blood – Not At All Simple
A long, strange trip

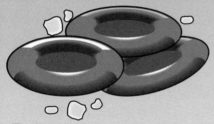

The little dots around the red blood cells are called platelets. When you get a cut, platelets move in and seal it up so that you don't lose all your blood. It's the first step in healing a wound.

Blood looks like some thick red liquid. But it is not. It's a clear liquid that has trillions of little cells floating in it. All kinds of them. This is a picture of red blood cells. There are about 25,000,000,000,000 (25 trillion) in each one of us. This picture is about 6,500 times bigger than real red blood cells. Each cell lives from 90 to 120 days and makes 150,000 trips through our entire body. Blood cells visit every other cell in our body, making deliveries and taking away waste.

Each kind of blood cell has a special job. Red blood cells deliver oxygen to other cells. They also take away carbon dioxide, which is one of the gases we exhale (or breathe out). The clear liquid the cells float in is called plasma (PLAZ-ma). The next time you see your doctor, ask to see some. Doctors usually love explaining things. Many doctors have a machine that spins blood samples. It separates the cells from the plasma.

Working Out

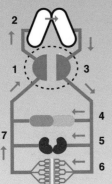

WHAT YOU NEED: A bicycle - a clock with a second hand

WHAT TO DO: Time your heartbeat for one minute. Ask someone in your family how to find your pulse. Ask thät person to explain it to you. Now take a very fast trip on your bicycle. Or take a hard run. As soon as you stop, count your pulse again. Pay attention to your mouth and to your breathing.

WHAT IS GOING ON: You took a trip and so did your blood. Your body needed more of what blood does.

Your pulse rate went up because your body needed more blood to do the work you made it do. The blood starts at your heart (**1**) and goes to your lungs (**2**) where it picks up oxygen and gets rid of carbon dioxide. It then goes back to the heart (**3**) where it is pumped to the intestines (**4**) where it picks up nutrients from the food you ate, through your kidneys (**5**) where waste is filtered out, through a miles-long network of tiny veins (**6**) that visit every single living cell in your body to make deliveries and carry away waste. It then goes back (**7**) to the heart (**1**) to start all over again. When you worked out, your body needed more food, more oxygen and it got hot. You breathed hard to bring in more oxygen and to let out some heat. You were probably breathing through your mouth, which is one of the places the body can get rid of extra heat. The trip you took wasn't nearly as long as the trip you put your blood through.

21

Dear Beakman,

Why is the sky blue?

Geoffrey

Dear Geoffrey,

That's a question that most everyone wonders about. But few people really go out and ask the question. When someone—like you—actually does something that a lot of people won't bother to, we say that person has initiative (in-ISH-e-tiv). It's a good thing to have. *You Can* make a blue sky on a kitchen table. *You Can* also make a sunset when the sky is red or orange.

Beakman

Beakman

It's Not Just Blue!

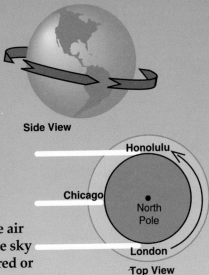

Side View

Look at the picture of the Earth. The arrows show how it spins. The top view shows how it would look from way above the North Pole looking down.

It's sunrise in Hawaii, noon in Chicago and sunset in England. Sunlight has to go through more air in the morning and evening. The sky is blue in Chicago. But it's also red or orange in Hawaii and England.

Honolulu

Chicago

North Pole

London

Top View

Sunlight Is all Colors

What looks like white light is really all colors mixed together. When the sun is straight up, the air scatters some of the blue light. That is what we see—scattered blue light, and it makes the sky look blue.

Afternoon in San Francisco is sunset in New York, where the light has to travel through more air to get to the ground. That much air scatters out all the colors except reds and oranges.

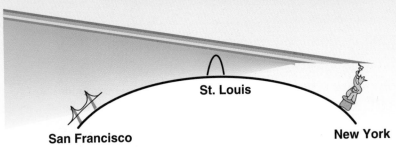

St. Louis

San Francisco

New York

Make a Sky in Your Kitchen

WHAT YOU NEED: Water - milk - flashlight - wide, clear glass bowl. (The bowl may be a bit hard to find. See if anyone on your street has a punch bowl. Sometimes people put flowers in a wide bowl. Either will do.)

WHAT TO DO: Wait until it's dark. Fill the bowl with water and 10 to 15 drops of milk. Shine your flashlight down from the top. Now shine the light from the side and look straight at it from the other side of the bowl.

WHAT IS GOING ON: You just made a model of the sky. Light from above turned the water light blue. From the side the water was red and orange. The milk acted like the air and scattered the blue light.

Even though the sky looks blue most of the time, clean, dry air is colorless. Smog is sometimes called photo-chemical pollution. Sunlight changes chemicals in the pollution and turns it brown.

Dear Beakman,

I am interested in how a camera works. Would you please explain? Thank you.

Mike

Dear Mike,

The best way to learn about cameras is to build one big enough to put your head inside. That way *You Can* take a look around and see what's going on. Really.

Beakman

First, a Little History

World's first photograph

More than 150 years ago, in 1824, a man in the nation of France took this picture. His name was Joseph Niépce. The picture is hard to see. It was taken from an attic window and is a photo of the roof across the yard. Several other rooftops can be seen. The important thing about this picture is that it was the first time anyone was able to get a photo to last. Before this picture, photographs were experimental and they kept disappearing. The invention was not a mega hit. Niépce died flat broke. He spent all of his money on his experiments.

EXPERIMENT #1

Get Inside a Camera

WHAT YOU NEED: Large cardboard box (make sure it can close) - masking tape - aluminum foil - nail - white paper - large bath towel

WHAT TO DO: Find the big box at a supermarket. Tell the people at the market that you need the empty box for science. They will think that's a good idea and say yes. Tape the white paper inside like in the drawing. Cut a 1 inch by 1 inch hole in the opposite side of the box and tape a piece of foil over it. Use the nail to punch a hole in the foil. Close the box and tape it all up. Tape down foil to seal the cracks. It is very important that no light at all get in the box—except through the little hole in the foil. Seal all corners and cracks. The darker the box is, the better this experiment works!

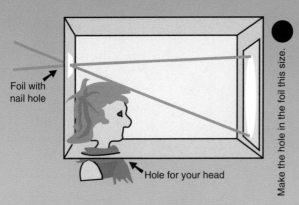

Foil with
nail hole

Hole for your head

Make the hole in the foil this size.

MORE STUFF TO DO: Look at the drawing and notice where the hole for your head is. Cut one in your box. Peek inside to see if there are light leaks. Seal them up. Take your box outside and wrap a big towel around your neck. This will keep out light. Now put the box over your head and look at the white paper. Move around and point the back of the box in different directions. You should have quite a show inside. If there are friends with you, ask them to move around. Give them a turn inside the box. The whole thing is too radical to keep for yourself.

WHAT IS GOING ON: You just made a kind of camera. It is called a camera obscura (ob-SCER-ah). The images you saw on the paper were upside down. That's how it is in all cameras. In a photographic camera, the white paper would be a piece of film that changes its chemistry when light hits it. In a video camera the white paper would be a device called a CCD—which stands for Charged Coupled Device. It turns light into an electrical signal. The nail hole in the foil is the lens. If

you had a friend cover it with his or her finger, that would be the shutter. Shutter speed is a way to change how long it is open. The speed of film is an ASA or ISO number. It tells how fast the film reacts to light. The lower the number, the more light you need. The f-stop changes how big the hole behind the lens is. The higher the f-stop number, the smaller the hole.

A movie camera takes 24 different pictures every second. Thomas Edison figured out the best way to move the film that fast. He punched holes on the edge of the film. They are called sprocket holes.

Dear Zak,

Candles were really an improvement on oil lamps. Candles didn't spill. The oil that burns in a candle is a solid. It changes into a liquid when it gets warmer near the flame. ⚠ NEVER, ever light a candle without permission from a grown-up. Fire from candles can burn you and your family — and your home.

Beakman

Beakman

28

Solids Or Liquids

WHAT YOU NEED: Can of chicken soup – refrigerator

WHAT YOU DO: Put the can of soup in the fridge for 1 hour. Take it out and *don't* shake it or turn it over. Open the can and take a look at what's floating on top of the soup. Warm up the soup. What's floating on top now? Have lunch. A little chicken soup never hurts.

WHAT'S GOING ON:

The blobs on top of the cold soup are chicken fat. Another word for it is *schmaltz*. It's solid when cold and liquid when warm. It's the light yellow pools floating in your bowl. *All animal fats will burn* – even schmaltz. But schmaltz never gets hard. It's mushy. That's why we say that mushy music is schmaltzy.

SO WHAT: Animal fats and plant oils that get real hard when they're solid are used to make candles. We call those things waxes. Wax comes from trees, crude oil, honeycombs and even berries. They're called candleberries.

29

Throw a Little Light on Things

Candles are ancient. Thousands of years ago, the best candles were made out of beeswax. Only a few people had them because beeswax was rare. Look at a honeycomb when you go shopping. It looks like this design.

The candles most people used were made out of animal fat. It's called tallow. The Pilgrims would have put tallow candles on the first Thanksgiving table. The Pilgrims made candles by saving the fat from the animals they raised to eat. They cooked it down and dipped strings into it. To make a hand-dipped candle, you have to dip the string into the wax or tallow about 125 times.

See if your family would like candles on your dinner table. They'll make it special.

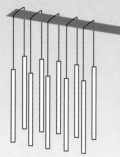

Strings are draped over a stick, then dipped in the tallow or beeswax. After cooling, it's dipped again and again until a candle is built up.

A cross-section of a dipped candle has rings like a tree.

In the 1700's people made candles from spermaceti (spur-MA-set-ee). It was fat in the head of sperm whales. It's one of the reasons people hunted and killed whales. The good news is that now most candles are made from paraffin wax, which is made from crude oil – not whales.

Dear Beakman,

How do they put music in a cassette tape?

Brandon

Dear Brandon,

Music, video and computer tape is sometimes called magnetic tape. That means the coating on the tape is changed when it passes over a magnet. The magnet is special. Its strength can change. It is called an electromagnet. *You Can* make an electromagnet to learn how your tape recorder works.

Beakman

Beakman

Examining a Cassette

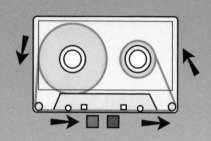

WHAT YOU NEED:
A cassette - a cassette recorder

WHAT TO DO: Look at the cassette and compare it to the drawing. See how the tape inside rolls across the open front? Look at the recorder. The little boxes in the drawing are the recorder's electromagnets. The red one is a recording head. The play-back head is the blue.

WHAT IS GOING ON: When the tape rolls past the recording head the electromagnet inside it changes tiny particles on the tape. They are moved into patterns. When you play back the tape the patterns change the play-back head. An electrical signal changes its strength as the patterns go by. The tape recorder makes them louder. And that is the music.

Making an Electromagnet

WHAT YOU NEED: A flashlight battery - 2 feet of bell wire - a nail - paperclip

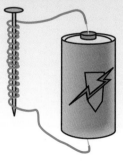

WHAT TO DO:
Wrap the wire around the nail so that it looks like the drawing. Take the plastic off the ends of the wire and hold them on the top and bottom of the battery. Hold the nail beside a paperclip and try to lift it up.

Note: You may have to visit a hardware store to find the wire. If you cannot go shopping, thin speaker wire will do.

WHAT IS GOING ON: When electricity goes along a wire, it has a magnetic field. It acts just like a refrigerator magnet. When you wrap the wire into a coil, you put all that magnetism together and it gets stronger. It is so strong it can pick things up like a regular magnet does.

See the Magnetic Field

WHAT YOU NEED:

The electromagnet you just made - white paper - hacksaw - steel nail - a grown-up friend - safety glasses/goggles

WHAT TO DO: ⚠ Put on the glasses or goggles. Hold the nail over the paper and use the hacksaw to cut a groove in it. Save the dust that falls on the paper. Do this many times. Take turns with your friend. Electromagnets are also in speakers and headphones, TVs, motors and telephones. How many electromagnets do you think there are in your house?

Make a little pile of the dust in the middle of the paper and hold it over your electro-magnet. Tap the paper gently until shapes

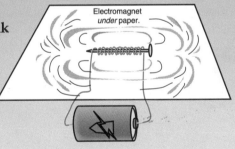

Electromagnet *under* paper.

happen. Carefully fold up the paper with the dust inside and throw it away. ⚠ It can be dangerous.

WHAT IS GOING ON: The shape you see is the same shape as the magnetic field. Your cassette recorder works just like this on a very small scale. The magnetic field changes shape when the amount of electricity changes. Those changes are recorded as the magnetic tape goes past the recording head in your cassette machine. The tape can now hold sounds, music, video or computer information.

Dear Beakman,

Sometimes a kitten's nose is dry and other times it's wet. Why?

Keri

Dear Keri,

Sometimes grown-ups don't pay attention to very special things. We say they *take them for granted*.

You asked a great question – one that I took for granted until you asked. First of all, it's wrong to think that you can tell if a cat or dog is sick just by the wetness of its nose. When its nose is wet, it's sweat.

Beakman

Beakman

Examining Things

WHAT YOU NEED: Cat or dog - magnifying glass

WHAT TO DO: With the magnifier, look at your pet's nose and at the pads on its feet. Compare them. Be gentle.

WHAT IS GOING ON: Both the nose and the feet pads are rough and very wrinkled. The wrinkles are there to increase the surface area. *You Can* learn more about that in Experiment #2.

Cats and dogs sweat for about the same reasons we do—stress, heat or fever. That can make the nose wet. Another thing: Only very exceptional people can lick their own nose. Cats and dogs do it all the time. That can make their noses wet, too.

In the feet pads and the nose are organs that release sweat. They are called eccrine glands (EK-creen). Humans have them, too – under our arms.

This is a picture of Beakman's cat, Algebra (AL-ja-BRA). He is an ornery cat named after a kind of math that solves several problems at once. Algebra the cat is several problems, too.

Wrinkled Noses

WHAT YOU NEED: A towel

WHAT TO DO: Lay the towel out flat on the floor. Notice how much of the floor it's covering. The top of the towel is its surface area. Now scrunch up the towel so that it fits in a space half that size. You'll have to make wrinkles in the towel to do it.

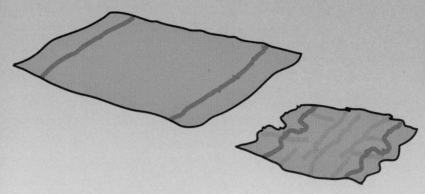

WHAT IS GOING ON:

The scrunched up towel takes up half the space but has the same surface area of the flat towel. The reason your cat or dog's feet and nose are all wrinkled is that more surface area helps the sweat evaporate better. It has to come out of their skin. The wrinkles pack more skin into a small space.

Dear Beakman,

What is chocolate? How do you make it?

Emily

Dear Emily,

Chocolate was first discovered and used by the ancient Mayans in Mexico. It was so valuable, they used it for money.

Chocolate is made by crushing the seeds of the cacao tree into a thick goo. The goo flavors all chocolate products—from chocolate kisses to ice cream.

The word chocolate is from the Mayan language, and it means sour water. That's because chocolate without added sugar is surprisingly bitter.

Beakman

Beakman

Make Some Mayan Chocolate

EXPERIMENT #1

Grown-ups love chocolate as much as you do. Some of them will even admit it. *You Can* make a kind of chocolate that is a lot like a kind of chocolate still popular in Mexico today.

WHAT YOU NEED: Dry, unsweetened cocoa - sugar - shortening - microwave oven - aluminum foil

WHAT TO DO: Visit the grocery store to get the cocoa powder. Taste a bit of it, and you'll see why the Mayans named it after something that tastes sour.

Put 3 level tablespoons of the powder in a bowl. Add 2 tablespoons of sugar and $1^1/2$ tablespoons of shortening. ⚠ Put the bowl in the microwave and zap it on high for 2 minutes. Stop the oven every 30 seconds and stir it up really well with a fork. After you take it out, keep stirring.

Spoon out the paste onto a piece of foil that you have put on a plate. If you like, smoosh it into the shape of a heart.

Stick it in the fridge for 30 minutes. Peel off the foil and eat it. Or better still, give it to someone as a gift.

WHAT IS GOING ON: Your chocolate is not milk chocolate. Milk chocolate is a lot finer and isn't gritty. That's because huge machines grind it up into a fine paste with dried milk.

The ancient Mayans lived in the Yucatan. The Maya people still live there today.

Chocolate Words

CACAO (ka-KAU-o)—The tree that grows cacao beans. Cacao beans (or seeds) grow in a big pod like a long cantaloupe.

CHOCOLATE LIQUOR—After the seeds are scooped out of their pod, they are set in the sun. Then they are ground up. The thick, gooey liquid they make is chocolate liquor. It's 54% fat.

COCOA (KO-ko)—Chocolate liquor is put in a huge press and the fat is squeezed out. The powder that's left is cocoa.

COCOA BUTTER—The fat in the cacao seeds/beans. It is thick, which is why it's called a butter.

MILK CHOCOLATE—Cocoa, cocoa butter, milk solids and sugar.

Chocolate is hard to make because the fat and the powder don't mix very well. Milton Hershey found out that if you add another ingredient – lecithin – the chocolate gets smooth. Hershey invented the chocolate kiss, which his mother used to wrap with foil. She was a very busy woman.

Dear Beakman,

How do things get their colors?

Dennis

Dear Dennis,

Different colors are really different kinds of light. We see colors because different things reflect or absorb different waves of light. Here is an experiment *You Can* do to learn about colors. Thanks for writing!

Beakman

Beakman

Taking White Light Apart

WHAT YOU NEED: Shallow pan - water - mirror - white paper - strong sunshine. *Or, a prism and sunshine*

WHAT TO DO:
Fill the pan with water and put it in the sun. Slide the mirror into the pan and sit it against the side of the pan. Wait for the water to get very still and smooth. Gently adjust the mirror up and down until you see a rainbow.

WHAT IS GOING ON:
Different colors of light have different wavelengths. Red light waves are longer than blue. The water above the mirror is triangle-shaped and makes the light break up by what size wavelength it has.

A prism or a clear window crystal will do the same thing!

With your experiment or with a prism, you took white light apart into its different colors!

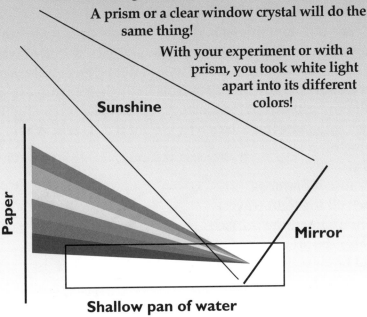

Sunshine

Paper

Mirror

Shallow pan of water

41

Light and the Universe
This is going to sound cosmic because it is!

The light we can see is a set of waves. Other waves are radio waves, x-rays and infrared energy. If you arrange the waves by their size, you get something called the electromagnetic spectrum. Light is just a very small part of it. Light from the sun looks white. But it is really all colors mixed together.

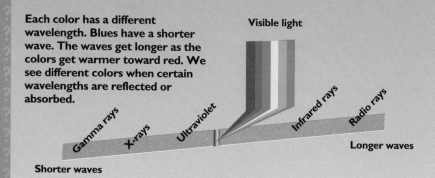

Each color has a different wavelength. Blues have a shorter wave. The waves get longer as the colors get warmer toward red. We see different colors when certain wavelengths are reflected or absorbed.

Visible light

Gamma rays

X-rays

Ultraviolet

Infrared rays

Radio rays

Longer waves

Shorter waves

So What

We see different things in different colors because the things they are made out of absorb or bounce back different waves of light. Without light, a leaf would not be green. The leaf is green only because the chemicals in the leaf absorb every color of light except for green. A leaf bounces green light back into our eyes. That's why we see it as green. When something is white, it is because it bounces back all the light waves. When something is black, it absorbs all waves of light and bounces back nothing.

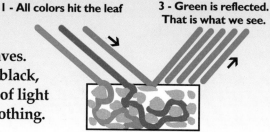

1 - All colors hit the leaf

3 - Green is reflected. That is what we see.

2 - The leaf absorbs every color except green.

Dear Beakman,

How do comics get their colors?

Mark

Dear Mark,

All the colors in the Sunday funnies are made from only four different colored inks. Each ink is printed one at a time on top of each other, and the colors mix.

Grab the Sunday funnies. You'll need them for the experiment *You Can* do to learn about comics in color.

Beakman

Beakman

Fooling the Brain

WHAT YOU NEED: Color comics - clear tape - water *Optional: Magnifying glass*

WHAT TO DO: Find the color green in the Sunday funnies. Cover it with tape. Press it down tight. Put one drop of water on top. Now look closely at the green through the water. Try it with other colors.

Grass green is 35% cyan (si-ANN) and 50% yellow. Magnified, it looks something like this.

WHAT IS GOING ON: The drop of water acted like a little magnifying glass, and the dots seem bigger. Newspapers aren't supposed to fool us. But printing does. Our brains get fooled. We can't see the dots as separate things, so cyan (light blue) and yellow dots get mixed together, and we see green. Now try the tape and water drops with Calvin and Hobbes or Blondie or Cathy or other color comics.

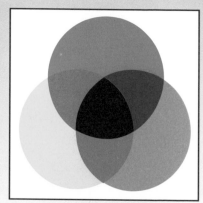

The inks are transparent. The colors mix and we get new colors.

It's All Done With Little Dots

Color printing uses little dots of just four colors to make all the colors you see. Look very closely at this chart. The dots are so big at the left that they touch. When they get smaller, the color gets weaker.

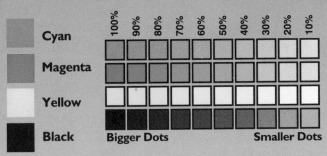

	100%	90%	80%	70%	60%	50%	40%	30%	20%	10%
Cyan										
Magenta										
Yellow										
Black										

Bigger Dots   **Smaller Dots**

Putting It Together

At the printing plant, printers put each color on separately. The rainbow pattern below is Beakman's tie. It's made by sending a piece of paper through a press that first puts on cyan, then magenta, then yellow and lastly, black. By themselves the separate inks don't look like much. Together, they look great. CMYK is printer talk for color. The K stands for black.*

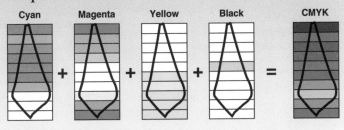

Cyan   +   Magenta   +   Yellow   +   Black   =   CMYK

*I know the word **Black** doesn't start with the letter **K**. But in a printing plant, **K** still means the color **Black**. The reason it's not **B**, is that **B** might be confused with the color **Blue**. The letter **K** doesn't turn up in the name of any other color. That's why **K** stands for black.

Dear Beakman,

Why can you remember dreams sometimes, and sometimes you can't?

Christine

Dear Christine,

We create dreams. They don't just happen to us. Dreams are things we make for ourselves. I know it doesn't always seem like that. But it's true. We make dreams. Dreams and dreaming are not fully understood. Perhaps we never will fully understand dreams. And that wouldn't be so bad. After all, a little mystery in life is a good thing.

Beakman

Beakman

The Subconscious Mind

This Is Going to Sound Cosmic

Within each of us are several ways of thinking. When we are awake and aware and in control of things, we are using our conscious (KAHN-shes) mind. This is the part of our mind that senses time and the physical world in which we live. There are different levels of the conscious mind. There is also another mind that is altogether different.

Working in the background all day long is the subconscious (sub-KAHN-shes) mind. It is not limited by things like the flow of time or the physical world. It's storing things in our memories and making comparisons with old memories all the time.

When we sleep, our conscious mind loses much of the control it has when we're awake. That leaves the subconscious mind to process all the things it's working with. The result is a lot like a movie that one part of our mind makes for another. But there are important differences. Dreams that you know you're dreaming are great places to get ideas. Mozart wrote some of his classical music after dreaming what it sounded like. The author Robert Louis Stevenson got ideas for books and stories from his dreams.

Remembering Dreams

EXPERIMENT #1

WHAT YOU NEED: Pencil and paper
Optional: Tape recorder

WHAT TO DO: Keep the paper and pen beside your bed. As soon as you wake up, write down the first thing that comes into your mind. If you're taping, just start talking. If you wake up in the middle of the night, do the same thing. Don't worry about your notes making sense. Don't look at them for a while.

WHAT IS GOING ON: Look at your notes the next afternoon. They still might not make sense. But if you relax and be peaceful with yourself, some pieces of your dreams will come back to you.

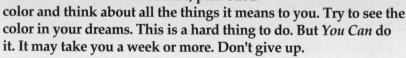

As you woke up, your conscious mind took over again. There was a better connection to your subconscious mind, and that's what ended up in your notes. Later, they became a kind of key to help you remember.

Directed Dreaming

EXPERIMENT #2

WHAT YOU NEED: Just yourself

WHAT TO DO: At bedtime, pick out a color and think about all the things it means to you. Try to see the color in your dreams. This is a hard thing to do. But *You Can* do it. It may take you a week or more. Don't give up.

WHAT IS GOING ON: You will see the color in the dream because you wanted it to be there. This is the difference between a dream and a movie. *You Can* be aware of being in a dream while you are dreaming. If you concentrate on this, you will be able to learn things and get ideas in dreams. If you weren't able to pick a color and make it appear in your dream, you just need to lighten up and give yourself more time.

Dear Beakman,

Why do people fart?

Bert

Dear Bert,

This is one of those rude-word-questions that I might get in trouble for talking about. Still it's an excellent question – one lots of people wonder about. The polite word for it is flatulence (FLA-chu-lentz). There are usually polite words for impolite subjects. It makes some of us feel better to have them around, even if we don't use them much. Flatulence is mostly air mixed with the gas methane. Other gases mixed in are the stuff that make farts smell. Methane doesn't smell. Really.

Beakman

Beakman

49

Sometimes It's Loud – Sometimes It Isn't

EXPERIMENT #1

WHAT YOU NEED: Just yourself

WHAT TO DO: Hold your lips tight together – as tight as *You Can*. Take a big breath. Now fill up your cheeks with the air. Keep pressing with your lungs while you try to keep your lips shut. What happened? Now try it again only relax your lips.

WHAT IS GOING ON:

There are ring-shaped muscles all along our digestive system. They open and close all the time without our knowing about it. They are called sphincters (SFINK-turs). It is a proper word, but it still makes grown-ups squirm. So don't use it around them. If you hold those ring muscles tight, it'll be loud when you pass gas. If your ring muscles are relaxed it will be quiet.

Stuff to Do to Understand

EXPERIMENT #2

WHAT TO DO: Brush your teeth.

WHY: The tooth paste is pushed along the tube and out to your brush. That's how food and gas move through our digestive system.

WHAT TO DO: Use the hose to wash your car.

WHY: The hose will spurt when you first turn it on. The water is pushing out air just like your body pushes out gas.

We're All Long Tubes

This is a simple drawing of our insides. You might say these are our guts. The first thing that makes gas is our stomach. We make acids there to start breaking down food. Pour some vinegar on a bit of baking soda. It will make gas a lot like our stomach does. That gas is a burp.

By the time food gets to our intestines, it is a paste. Microbes that live in our intestines start breaking down the paste that hasn't yet been absorbed by our body. When microbes do that, methane gas is made. The bad smell comes from foods that contain chemicals like sulfur – like eggs, onions and beans. The blue dashes in the drawing are pockets of gas forming in our guts. It has to go somewhere. It gets pushed out our rear end.

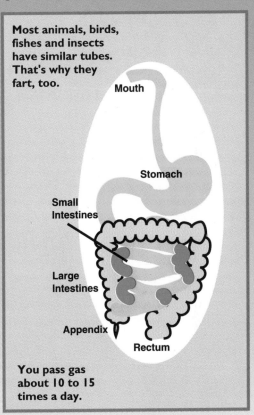

Most animals, birds, fishes and insects have similar tubes. That's why they fart, too.

Mouth

Stomach

Small Intestines

Large Intestines

Appendix

Rectum

You pass gas about 10 to 15 times a day.

The gas you cook or heat with was made the same way our body makes gas. The Earth has pockets of gas made by microbes that digested plants and animals millions of years ago. I guess when they call it natural gas, they're right.

Dear Beakman,

Why do feet smell?

Hank

Dear Hank,

Feet smell and feet sometimes smell bad. Feet smell because animals, including humans, produce chemicals that identify us as individuals. They are called pheromones (FAIR-eh-moans). Feet smell bad when very tiny plants or animals grow on our skin. It sounds gross, but it's true. They are called microbes (MY-kroabs), which means small life. They are everywhere and *You Can* grow some at home.

Beakman

Beakman

We All Have Our Own Unique Smell

WHAT YOU NEED: A friend - a blindfold - a quiet time - permission from your family

WHAT TO DO: Sit down in the living room and put on the blindfold. Don't peek. Tell your friend to go around the house and take a T-shirt out of everyone's clothes dresser – one each for every member of your family. You should stay quiet and get relaxed. Your friend will let you smell each shirt. Without touching the shirts, *You Can* still tell whose shirt it is just by the smell. Now try it at your friend's house.

The nose knows!

WHAT IS GOING ON: We all have our own unique smell – something that is ours alone and different from anyone else. We get used to these smells and don't think about it much. That's why you should relax and be quiet when you do this. Our smells even change the fragrance of perfume or cologne. That's why it's a little different on every person. It's also the reason different houses smell different. The smell comes from the pheromones we make.

The Unseen World

There are plants and animals so small we need a microscope to see them. There are billions and billions of them, and they live everywhere – even on us. They even live inside us.

The microbes that make feet smell bad have very long names. One is called *Brevibacteria-linen*. Another is *Corybacteria JK*. They are both kind of like family names. Many microbes are members of those families, and when they grow they're smelly.

We can wash some of them off. But microbes duplicate on and on, so we can't ever get rid of them. When something has been cleaned of all microbes, we say that it's sterile. But microbes always get back in eventually. Microbes are just about everywhere – at least on this planet. We are protected from most of the bad ones by our bodies' immune systems.

53

Growing Microbes

WHAT YOU NEED: Clean mayonnaise jar - unflavored gelatin - cotton swab - water - patience

WHAT TO DO: Boil 1/2 cup water, sprinkle in 4 envelopes unflavored gelatin. Dissolve it. Pour into the mayonnaise jar and set the jar on its side. Let the extra pour out. Put on sneakers without socks and go play outside. Three hours later, the gelatin will be hard and your feet will be smelly. This is a great experiment to do at school. Collect your microbes after recess or gym. Take the swab and rub it well in between all your toes. Now carefully brush the gelatin with the cotton tip in long strokes. Close the jar and put it in a warm, dark spot. Leave it there 4 whole days. Go wash your feet.

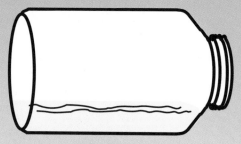

WHAT IS GOING ON: Inside your shoes it's dark, warm and damp – perfect for microbes! And they grow and grow. Your jar is pretty much the same. The gelatin is what the microbes are eating. It is called a growth medium. After 4 days, you'll be able to see grooves in the gelatin. The microbes are eating it. When you open it, you'll smell something much worse than smelly feet. It smells horrible. Really. Don't keep the jar any longer and don't touch it inside. Fill it with hot water, let it soak and then recycle the jar. Wash your hands!

Microbes grow even when we don't want them to. That's why the forgotten thing in the back of the refrigerator looks all gross, smelly and hairy. It is not a Science Fair project. It's microbes.

Dear Beakman,

How can a ship made of metal float? Steel and iron sink. But boats made out of them do not. Why?

Amber

Dear Amber,

It is a little hard to understand why steel or iron can be made into big ships. Yes, a chunk of steel is heavy and will sink in water. But steel is not as heavy as the water that the ship's hull pushes away, or displaces.

Here are the experiments *You Can* do to learn how they make boats out of steel that float.

Beakman

Beakman

Pushing Water Away: Displacement

WHAT YOU NEED: Big jar or bowl - soda bottle - water - marking pen

WHAT TO DO: Fill the jar half full of water. Make a mark on the jar where the top of the water is. Fill the soda bottle half full of water and mark it, too. Push the soda bottle down into the jar. Push down until the top of the water in the bottle meets the top of the water in the jar. Look at the marks you made. See if they still match the top of the water in both the soda bottle and the big jar.

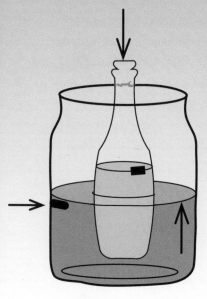

WHAT IS GOING ON: Your soda bottle pushed away the water in the big jar. That is why the water line moved up. The water in the soda bottle stayed the same. Feel how heavy the soda bottle and its water are. Anything the same size that weighs less will float. Anything heavier will sink.

Floating

WHAT YOU NEED: Bucket - aluminum foil - water - hammer

WHAT TO DO: Fill the bucket with water. Make a little boat with the foil and put it on the water. What happened? Take the foil out of the water and make it into a little ball. Then take it outside to a sidewalk and hammer the ball until you cannot make it any smaller. Fold it over and hammer it more. Put the little foil ball in the water. What happens?

WHAT IS GOING ON:

The little boat floated. That is because it was not as heavy as the water it pushed away. Then you made the foil smaller and it could not push away enough water to float. The ball weighed exactly the same as the boat. But it got so small it was heavier than the water it could push away. So it sank.

Even though a ship is very big and very very heavy, it is not as heavy as the water it pushes away. That is why a big ship made of steel can float! (Don't forget to use the water from your experiments for the plants outside.)

If you live near a lake or river, visit the docks to see the boats. Some boats are made of concrete which is heavy. The cement boats float because they weigh less than the water they push away.

In most libraries books about boats have the number 478.30. Check it out!

Dear Beakman,

How does gasoline make a car work? Would you explain?

Dan

Dear Dan,

Gasoline is one of those good news/bad news things. The good news is we can get a great deal of energy out of it. The bad news is gasoline can produce so much energy we are having a hard time finding a replacement that's as good that will not pollute. More bad news is that once we use up the gasoline that's available, there won't be any more. It is not renewable.

Beakman

Beakman

Here's a New Mantra for You

EXPERIMENT #1

WHAT YOU NEED: A bicycle

WHAT TO DO: Pick one of your feet to pay special attention to and take a ride. When you're riding, make a rhythm with these four words - *fuel, compress, power & exhaust.* When people meditate sometimes they use a mantra, which is words they say to themselves. Those four words are your bicycle mantra. They will help you understand how gasoline makes a car go. Be sure to make the rhythm with just one of your feet. The other foot is just along for the ride. Read more about it on the next page.

What in the world does this have to do with cars?

WHAT IS GOING ON: Even though your bicycle rolls, you power it by pushing down on your pedal. Most cars do the same thing. Metal blocks called pistons are pushed down when gasoline explodes. A piston is the same shape as an oatmeal box. Pistons fit inside tubes called cylinders (SIL-en-durs).

Explosions — That's How Gasoline Works

Most motors have 4, 6, 8 or even 12 pistons. The pistons move inside a cylinder. Each cylinder has at least 2 valves. When the fuel valve is open, the piston moves **DOWN** and sucks in a mist made of air and gasoline.

On your bike, this is the first count. Tell yourself *"fuel"* on the first pedal push down.

Fuel valve OPEN   Exhaust valve CLOSED

1

Both valves CLOSED

Next, both valves close and the piston moves **UP**. This squeezes the gasoline mist into a very small space. This is called compression. On your bike, tell yourself *"compress"* on the first stroke upward.

2

Both valves CLOSED

Now comes the explosion! With both valves still closed, the spark plug makes a spark which detonates the gasoline. It expands with a lot of force and pushes the piston **DOWN**.

On your bike, tell yourself *"power"* on the second stroke down. Push extra hard on the pedal.

3

Fuel valve CLOSED   Exhaust valve OPEN

Next, the exhaust valve opens, the piston moves **UP** and pushes all the burnt gasoline vapor out into the air. The motor has to get rid of it to start with the first cycle all over again. The exhaust is air pollution. On your bike, tell yourself *"exhaust"* on the second stroke upward.

4

The cylinders and pistons in your car can be arranged differently. This is a V. If someone has a V-8, their car has eight pistons arranged in a V pattern.

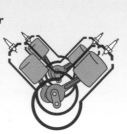

This is called an in-line or straight engine.

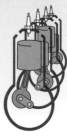

Dear Beakman,

I would like to know how you can make glass out of sand. Sand is not clear but glass is. How come?

Lauren

Dear Lauren,

Glass is a shining miracle of human achievement. It was first made 3,500 years ago in Iraq and Egypt. Sometimes things don't seem clear at first. That is true for an idea or a lesson. And it is true for glass, too. *You Can* make something like glass at home. You will need help from an adult because you will work with things that are hot and dangerous.

Beakman

Beakman

61

Make Break-Away Glass

In the movies sometimes people fall through a window. That would hurt - bad. So, they use fake glass. It's called break-away glass because it cracks so easily. It is made out of sugar.

Just like sand, sugar does not look clear. When it is heated and allowed to cool, all the little pieces melt together. We say it fuses.

This experiment is like a recipe in candy making. You must have an adult do it. If they say no, tell them you want them to explain something to you. They usually like doing that. If that doesn't work try telling them it would be fun. Or, save this for school. This can be done in a classroom with a hotplate. *Make sure an adult helps you do this experiment!*

⚠ *CAUTION: Do not touch the melted sugar. It is very hot. It could cause bad burns.*

WHAT YOU NEED: Sugar - light corn syrup - water pie pan - cooking oil - ice water - measuring cup - tablespoon - heavy sauce pan *OPTIONAL: candy thermometer*

WHAT TO DO: Boil 1/2 cup water in the sauce pan. Add 1 cup sugar, 5 tablespoons corn syrup. Stir. Bring to boil covered. Uncover. With no stirring at all, on high heat bring to 310°. That temperature is called *hard crack*. It will take about 6-8 minutes boiling. To check for hard crack, let a drop of the mixture fall into a glass of ice water. Look close. When it makes a fine clear thread that breaks, it is hot enough. ⚠ *Remove from heat quickly.* If it gets too hot, your glass will turn brown.

Lightly brush the pie pan with oil. Make sure it does not pool. Pour the sugar mixture in the pie pan. Put it in the refrigerator for 30 minutes. When it is completely cool, pop the glass out of the pie pan.

WHAT IS GOING ON: Your break-away glass will be clear even though you made it out of sugar which doesn't look clear.

Sugar and sand both melt. They both fuse. And both really are clear. Little scratches and little nicks make sand and sugar look white.

The melted sugar will look like this at 310° - hard crack.

When we melt either sugar or sand, they can cool with a smooth shiny surface and we can see light come through. In most libraries the best place to read about glass is the encyclopedia. Check it out!

If you boil orange peels and take them out before adding the sugar, your break-away glass becomes a very large orange-flavored lollipop - so big you need to share it with several friends!

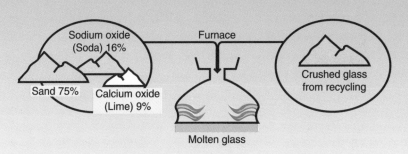

Sometimes miracles can be explained and still be miracles. Glass is one of them. Windows, eyeglasses, insulation, mirrors, tubing, even fiber optic telephone cables are all made out of glass. Glass can be used over and over again and it doesn't rot. It's pretty cool that glass is mostly sand, melted in a big furnace!

63

Dear Beakman,

What are hiccups? Where do they come from?

Elizabeth

Dear Elizabeth,

Hiccups happen to everyone, and they aren't always much fun. A little hiccup is a big reminder that we aren't always in control of our own body. The word *hiccup* is special, too. It's an onomatopoeia (an-o-mah-to-PEE-ah). That means it's a word that imitates a sound. *Hiccup* is a pretty good imitation of the actual sound a hiccup makes. Words like *bang, hiss* and *poof* are also onomatopoeias.

Beakman

Beakman

Normal Breathing

Hiccups happen when normal breathing gets messed up.
Here's what normal breathing is like:

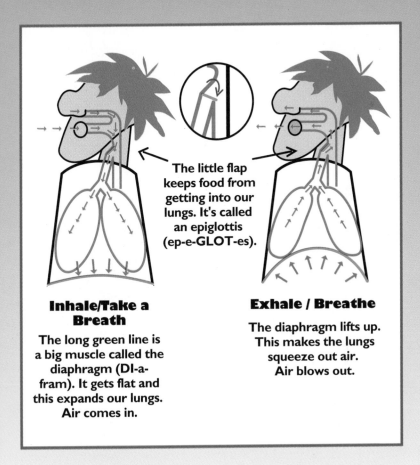

The little flap keeps food from getting into our lungs. It's called an epiglottis (ep-e-GLOT-es).

Inhale/Take a Breath

The long green line is a big muscle called the diaphragm (DI-a-fram). It gets flat and this expands our lungs. Air comes in.

Exhale / Breathe

The diaphragm lifts up. This makes the lungs squeeze out air. Air blows out.

Ask different people what they do to cure hiccups. You'll get lots of different answers. No one cure can be guaranteed to work for you. My favorite is to put peanut butter on the roof of my mouth and eat it really slowly.

Putting the Hic in Hiccups

WHAT YOU NEED: Tube from toilet paper - tape - aluminum foil

WHAT TO DO: Cut a hole in the side of the tube and tape a flap of foil over the hole like a little door. It should look like the picture.

Hold the tube up to your mouth, cover the other end with your hand and breathe in gently. Now breathe in real hard. What happened?

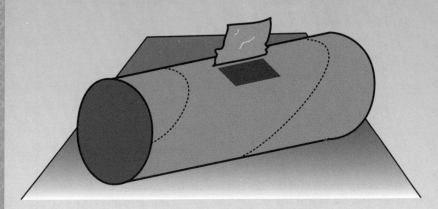

WHAT IS GOING ON: The little foil flap slammed shut, which is the same thing happening when you hiccup. Hiccups happen when the diaphragm has a spasm (SPAZ-em). It just starts moving up and down quickly and out of control. Little spasms happen to a lot of muscles.

When the diaphragm gets one, air is sucked in very fast and our little flap – the epiglottis – slams shut. That's what makes the sound. The only cure for the hiccups is to somehow relax the diaphragm and get it back on track breathing normally.

Dear Beakman,

What are optical illusions?

Abby

Dear Abby,

What you see is not always what you get. We learn to perceive—or understand—what we're looking at. Sometimes our brains get clues wrong. Other times, our brains fill in the missing pieces. Our brains cause optical illusions in both ways. The optical illusion you see the most is probably television. TV doesn't really move. Television is really lots of still pictures that are shown to us very quickly. Our brain puts the images together because it has learned to expect the movement.

Beakman

Beakman

A Famous Illusion

Back in 1915, a cartoonist named W.E. Hill first published this drawing. It's hard to see what it's supposed to be. Is it a drawing of a pretty young girl looking away from us? Or is it an older woman looking down at the floor? Well, it's both. The key is perception and what you expect to see. Here's a hint: The young girl's necklace is the older woman's mouth. The young girl's chin and jaw are the older woman's nose.

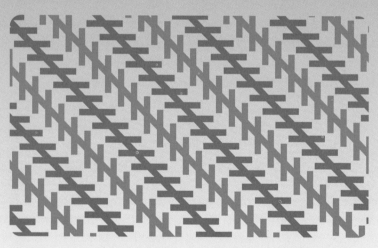

Are the longest lines parallel, or are they closer to each other at one end? They look crooked but are not. Measure them. They can even look curved. Your brain is fooling around again.

BEAKMAN

You Can tell what this says because you know what it's supposed to say. I always sign my letters with my name. You fill in the missing parts with your brain. Look at the shapes below. Do you see a square (**1**) triangles (**2**) and circles (**3**)? You might even see several, and some of them are brighter than others. None of it's really there. You're used to seeing them. Your mind just filled in the blanks. They are illusions, too.

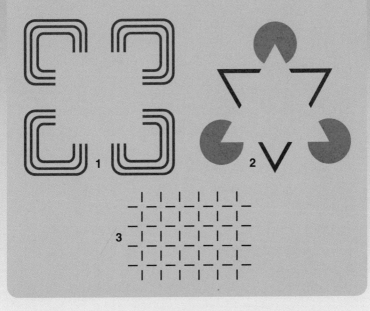

Look real closely at the color light green in the Sunday comics. That's an optical illusion, too. It's really little blue dots mixed with yellow dots. Our brains put the 2 together to get green.

Dear Beakman,

Do they make gelatin out of horse hooves?

Monika

Dear Monika,

That's a trick question! Usually people ask it to gross out someone. The best time to ask it is when someone is eating a big, bright gelatin dessert. The answer to your question, of course, is "Yes, one can make gelatin from a horse hoof." But gelatin can also be made from other animals and even seaweed. Gelatin is a solid protein that traps a liquid inside a network. So, a gelatin dessert is both a solid and a liquid. We call that a colloid (CALL-loyd). *You Can* prove it yourself with these experiments.

Beakman

Beakman

A Solid and A Liquid

EXPERIMENT #1

WHAT YOU NEED: Unflavored gelatin - apple juice - microwave oven - help from a grown-up

WHAT TO DO: Put 1 cup apple juice in a sauce pan. ⚠ Heat it just till it boils, then turn off the stove. Sprinkle in one envelope of the gelatin. Let it soften a minute and stir it in. Pour the liquid into a bowl and stick it in your refrigerator till it gets solid. Examine it. Touch it. Eat a spoonful. You just made an apple gelatin dessert. Now spoon out several chunks onto a plate and zap it in the microwave till you see liquid oozing out.

WHAT IS GOING ON: This dessert is a lot like a wet sponge. We eat both the sponge and the liquid that is in the sponge. The sponge is made from a protein found in many animal parts. It's even in us – in people. It is a solid that arranges itself in a pattern. Heat breaks down the pattern. When you chilled the apple juice/gelatin mixture, the pattern formed around little droplets of apple juice. It got trapped. The microwave added heat again, and the apple juice was freed to ooze out the bottom.

You Can do this with packaged gelatin dessert. I just wanted you to see that you can make a delicious food without having to buy something with a lot of sugar dumped in. Apple juice is plenty sweet by itself and is better for us.

A Closer Examination

If You Pay Closer Attention, an Everyday Event Can Become an Experiment

WHAT YOU NEED: A chicken dinner

WHAT TO DO: The next time your family roasts a chicken in the oven, serve it directly from the roasting pan. Leave the leftovers in the roaster, and after it cools, put the pan in the fridge. After it gets cold, you'll find chicken-flavored gelatin in the bottom of the pan.

WHAT IS GOING ON:

Gelatin is in the part of meat we call gristle (GRIS-ul). And it's in the crunchy stuff in between the bones. Gelatin forms in a pattern (#1). When it's heated, the pattern breaks up (#2). When it cools again, the pattern reforms and traps a droplet of chicken juice (#3). The same thing happens with gelatin dessert, except the liquid isn't chicken juice. It's a sweetened, flavored liquid. This experiment also works with turkey, beef or pork.

Any time one kind of matter traps another kind of matter we call it a colloid. Another colloid is whipped cream. It is a liquid (the cream) trapping a gas (the air you whip into the cream to fluff it up). Another colloid is paint, which is a solid (the pigment) suspended in a liquid.

Dear Beakman,

Why does a soda straw look bent in a glass of water?

Peter

Dear Peter,

You Can affect light and light beams several different ways. *You Can* bounce them, which is also called reflection. And *You Can* bend them, which is called refraction (re-FRAK-shun). Refraction is what happens with lenses of all kinds, from camera lenses to eyeglasses. It's also what's happening when you look through a glass of water at a straw.

There are lots of experiments *You Can* do to bend light. These 2 are my favorites. Find more at your library.

Beakman

Beakman

Water Is a Lens

WHAT YOU NEED:

Clear jar - water - shoe box - flashlight

WHAT TO DO: Cut two slits in one end of the box like in the drawing. At night, when it's very dark, put a jar of water in the box. Shine your flashlight through the slits. Watch what happens to the light beams.

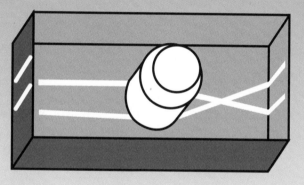

WHAT IS GOING ON:

The water bends the beams of light and they will criss-cross. If you put a magnifying glass or a lens in the box, the same thing will happen to the light. Water acts like a lens and bends – or refracts – light.

The next time you see a pond or a stream, look at the bottom through the water. The water will bend the light and make the bottom look much closer to you than it really is. Other liquids and even air also bend light. That's in Experiment #2.

Rates of Refraction

WHAT YOU NEED: Empty glass jar - water - rubbing alcohol - cooking oil - ruler - help and permission from your family ⚠ (Alcohol is dangerous.)

WHAT TO DO: Put about 2 inches of water in the jar. Tilt it to one side and gently pour in the same amount of oil. Tilt it back up. Now tilt it over again and gently add the rubbing alcohol. Pour slowly. When you straighten the jar, you'll see 3 separate layers. Stick in a ruler and look at it from the side. What happens?

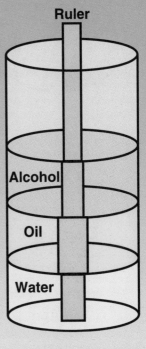

Ruler

Alcohol

Oil

Water

WHAT IS GOING ON:

The ruler was all different sizes. The oil bends light the most, and the ruler looked very big. Water bends light less, and the ruler wasn't enlarged as much. Alcohol enlarged the ruler some, but not as much as water.

You Can also bend light at the same time you reflect it. Look into a shiny spoon. You'll see yourself upside-down. The light criss-crossed and flipped your face upside-down.

Dear Kerri,

Lightning is a tremendous electrical spark. Sometimes it goes from one part of a cloud to another part. Sometimes the spark goes from one cloud to another. Still other times, it goes from a cloud to the ground. Lightning makes a lot of light and a lot of noise. The light travels faster than the noise does. *You Can* use that difference to measure the distance to a thunderhead.

Beakman

Beakman

EXPERIMENT #1

How Far Away Is the Lightning?

WHAT YOU NEED: A storm - wrist watch

WHAT TO DO: The next time you see the flash of lightning, start timing with your watch. Or, you can count the seconds slowly. Stop timing or counting as soon as you hear the thunder. Divide the number of seconds by the number 5. The answer is the number of miles you are from the lightning.

WHAT IS GOING ON:
Thunder and lightning happen together. But we sense them separately because of distance and speed. Light travels very, very fast. A beam of light could go to the moon and back in seconds. Sound would take weeks.* We see the light from the lightning as soon as it happens. That's when we start counting. The sound arrives later. It travels at about 1/5 mile per second.

* A sound wave could never really travel to the moon and back for a simple reason. Outer space is a vacuum – no air, no atmosphere. Sound needs something physical to move through. It can't go through a vacuum.

Lightning

Clouds in this shape make lightning. They are called cumulonimbus clouds (kyoom-u-lo-NIM-bus).

We can only guess where lightning comes from. When we have a guess with a lot of clues, we call that a theory (THEER-ee). One theory on lightning involves friction and static electricity. The top of this cloud can be miles high. Inside it, the air is moving very fast. Cold air is sinking. Warm air is rising. This causes friction, which causes static electricity. The top of the cloud has a positive charge(+). The bottom has a negative charge (–). Lightning is a huge spark that balances out the difference in charges.

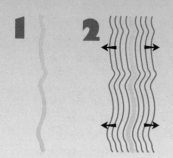

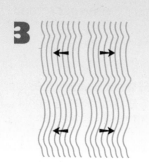

How It Happens

1 The lightning bolt connects a negatively and a positively charged area. It is very, very hot.

2 The heat makes the air expand. It moves very quickly.

3 The moving air makes sound waves. By now you have already seen the lightning. The sound waves are slower. You'll hear a bang and a rumble as they reach your ears.

Dear Beakman,

I am really interested in magnets.
I do not understand how the forces in magnets work.
Could you explain?

Joe

Dear Joe,

You Can do these experiments to start learning about magnets. But it is a big subject. Go to the library to learn more. Ask a librarian. They do not know everything. But they all know how to find out and they will help you find out.

Beakman

Beakman

First, Just Think About It

WHAT YOU NEED: An active imagination

WHAT TO DO: Imagine you have a piece of iron and you are cutting it in half. If you keep doing that the pieces will get so small you couldn't see them anymore. Because you are imagining this, you could keep cutting the piece in half until it got so small you would end up with an atom of iron. That's as small as you could go and still have iron.

WHAT IS GOING ON: This is one way of picturing an atom. Atoms are made of electrons (ee-LEC-tron), protons (PRO-ton) and neutrons (NU-tron). The electrons orbit the center of the atom, which is called the nucleus (NUK-lee-us). Magnetism comes from the electrons spinning while they circle the nucleus.

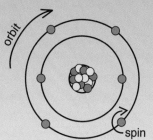

- ● Electron
- ● Proton
- ○ Neutron

The atom diagram is a picture of the element carbon. All living things on Earth are made partly of carbon. That includes us. It is also what diamonds are made of.

Make a Magnet

WHAT YOU NEED: Refrigerator magnet - 2 sewing needles ⚠️ *(Be careful with them!)*

WHAT TO DO: Hold the magnet in 1 hand and 1 needle in the other. Rub the magnet with the needle but rub it in 1 direction only. Do this 60 times. Now hold the needle next to the other needle and lift. What happened?

WHAT IS GOING ON: The electrons in the magnet are spinning in a similar direction. When you rubbed the needle against the magnet you changed the electrons in the needle. You realigned (ree-ah-LINED) them. They are now spinning in pretty much the same direction and that makes the needle a magnet. Magnetism is not a simple thing. But the spin of the electrons is a good place to start understanding.

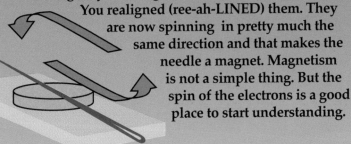

The Planet Earth Is a Magnet

WHAT YOU NEED: Cork - bowl of water -magnet/needle - dish soap

WHAT TO DO: ⚠ Have an adult slice the cork so that you have a piece that is 1/2 inch thick. Put one drop of dish soap in the center of the bowl of water. Put the needle on the cork and float it where you just put the soap. Gently spin the cork. Wait. What happened?

WHAT IS GOING ON: No matter which way you put the bowl, the needle will always point north. You just made a compass. Inside the Earth there is a lot of iron and the electrons in it are spinning in similar directions. The Earth is much bigger than your needle and is a very powerful magnet. It will always pull your compass to the same direction. 5,000 years ago a Chinese emperor named Huang-ti made the first compass.

Dear Beakman,

I am wondering how microwave ovens work.

Forrest

Dear Forrest,

A microwave oven uses radio waves to move molecules in food. That movement causes friction (FRICK-shun), which causes heat. You must have a grown-up help you with your experiments today. ⚠ A microwave oven can be very dangerous. No kidding.

Beakman

Beakman

What Is Friction?

WHAT YOU NEED: A wire coat hanger - the palms of your hands

WHAT TO DO: Put your hands together and start rubbing up and down real hard. Keep doing it until you feel a change. Now bend the bottom of the coat

⚠ CAUTION: This area gets HOT! Be careful.

hanger in half. Unbend it and then rebend it. Do this quickly 10 times. Then feel the bend in the wire. Be careful!

WHAT IS GOING ON: Both the palms of your hands and the wire got hot. The reason for that is the movement energy you put into them. The molecules in your hands and in the wire started moving. Molecules have to do something with the energy you put in. That energy is changed into heat.

But Water Doesn't Bend
Molecules are Moved by Microwaves

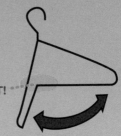

Positive end

Hydrogen

Hydrogen

Oxygen

Negative end

This is a picture of a water molecule.
It has 2 hydrogen atoms and 1 oxygen atom. That is why water is called H_2O. There are more electrons at the oxygen end of the atom, so it has a negative charge. The hydrogen end has a positive charge. The molecule will rotate when there is a change in the electrical field it is in. It behaves like a magnet does - rotating to match the magnetic field. Microwaves change the electrical field.

Your oven is a radio station
It Really Cooks!

All mixed up   **Lined up by the microwave**

Every time a wave goes by the molecules change the direction they point.

Inside your microwave is a device that sends out microwaves. They are set at a frequency that will affect water and fat molecules. They are the same microwaves we use to send long distance phone calls, satellite TV and radar. The waves change the electrical field and that causes the molecules to flip and spin. When they hit each other, friction causes heat.

This is a diagram of how a microwave behaves. It is not how microwaves look. The distance between the high points is the wavelength. The number of times a high point goes by is the frequency. The microwaves in your oven move very very fast. Between 1,000,000,000 (1 billion) and 5,000,000,000,000 (5 trillion) waves go by every second!

Metal Reflects Microwaves
A Problem for Cooks and for Jet Fighter Pilots

EXPERIMENT #2

WHAT YOU NEED:
Your microwave oven - a bag of microwave popcorn - a grown-up to help

COLD

HOT

Microwaves bounce off metal pots and metal airplanes

Microwaves are absorbed by chemicals in popcorn bags and Stealth airplanes

WHAT TO DO: Empty the popcorn out of the package. Put the empty popcorn bag in the oven and cook it for 30 seconds. Have an adult remove it. Without touching the bag, feel its temperature.

WHAT IS GOING ON: After it has cooled, take the bag apart and look at the material in the side of the bag. It is a special chemical that absorbs microwaves. It is also in some pizza boxes. The chemical is similar to the coating that is on a kind of airplane that radar cannot see. They are called Stealth aircraft. Radar is microwaves. A metal plane reflects them. The special chemical absorbs them and the plane cannot be detected as easily. ⚠️ *Do not put metal in your microwave!*

Dear Beakman,

What is the problem with the ozone layer? What is the ozone layer? What can I do about it?

Kelly

Dear Kelly,

Those are questions a lot of readers have. I get hundreds of letters asking about the ozone. Ozone is a word we see and hear a lot in the news. And the news can scare us.

I know that there is a lot of fear about the ozone. But *You Can* turn fear into something else. What you change fear into is up to you. But before *You Can* change fear, you have to understand what's going on. It's how you begin.

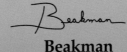

Beakman

What Is Ozone?

The circle drawings are the shape of an ozone molecule. Ozone is made up of oxygen atoms. The oxygen we breathe is made from 2 atoms. It's called O_2. Ozone is made from 3 atoms and is called O_3. Ozone isn't very stable. It can break apart and turn into O_2 easily. There is lots of it high above the Earth near the edge of outer space.

Ozone is the right size and shape to absorb energy from the sun that can be dangerous. The ozone forms a layer that absorbs some of the sun's energy. That layer protects us.

The dangerous sunlight is called UV, which is short for ultraviolet. Some of this light shines on us every day. The big fear is that more of it might hurt us. UV light can change a part of our skin cells. It can make them duplicate themselves like crazy, like a copying machine gone nuts. That's all skin cancer is – uncontrolled copying of skin cells.

The fear of more sickness is what we have to change into something else.That's a big job, and we all need help with it. Big jobs are a lot easier when we work together. This problem is something *You Can* bring to your class at school and to your friends and family.

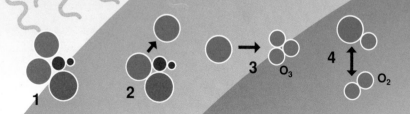

What Is the Problem?

To better understand the problem see the diagram on page 86. It shows how freon and other related chemicals drift up miles above the Earth to the part of our air called the stratosphere (STRAT-us-fear). That's where ozone is. When high energy sunlight (**1**) hits a freon molecule, it breaks up and releases a chlorine atom (**2**). The chlorine atom then bangs into an ozone molecule (**3**). That turns the ozone into regular oxygen (**4**). Regular oxygen (O_2) isn't the right size and shape to absorb the kind of sunlight that can be dangerous.

How Did All This Start?

A long time ago, refrigerators used a poisonous gas to move heat. Moving heat is how all refrigerators still work. The gas was ammonia gas, and it made refrigeration dangerous. Chemists worked very hard to invent a new gas that behaved like ammonia but wasn't poison. They invented freon (FREE-on), which is inert. Inert means it won't mix with anything else at all. It seemed perfect. People got to have refrigerators, and that was very good. But in the 1970s, scientists found out that if you add solar energy to a freon molecule it will split up. By then the gas was used in spray cans and to puff up plastic foam. People cut down on the use of freon. But they didn't stop using it. That's a problem.

FREON

SO WHAT: If you are concerned about the ozone layer, talk about it. Keep talking till someone listens. Someone will.

One of the things *You Can* change fear into is action. Use less plastic foam. Maybe get your class to write letters to our political leaders. Tell them how you feel. Or come up with something else on your own. You decide.

Dear Beakman,

Why does an onion make you cry when it's cut?

Bryan

Dear Bryan,

Onions have been stinging eyes for thousands of years. But it wasn't until the 1970s that a scientist from Albany, New York, figured out the puzzle of what's going on. He is named Eric Block. *You Can* do today's experiments only if a grown-up helps. That's because a knife is dangerous.

Beakman

Beakman

Pipes Connect Our Eyes and Nose

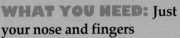

WHAT YOU NEED: Just your nose and fingers

WHAT TO DO: Hold your nose and mouth closed. Now blow air into your nose from your lungs. Sometimes we need to be gentle with ourselves. This is one of those times. Do not blow too hard. Pay attention to where air comes out.

Tear gland

Tear duct (to nose)

WHAT IS GOING ON: Our eyes are precious and delicate. Our body protects them with a constant bath that's always running. It's tears. Tears are made in a gland above our eyes. Every time we blink, we wash our eyes with tears. This could get messy, so the tears have a place to drain. It's a little pipe called a tear duct that drains the tears into our nose.

When you blew, air came out of your eyes. The air came up through the tear duct. That chemical the onion makes, the one with the long name, can go up the duct and get into our eyes. It can also drift directly into our eyes because it is a vapor and is in the air.

Whenever anything hurts our eyes, or gets into our eyes, the tear gland makes a lot more tears. It is trying to wash out our eyes.

When that onion chemical gets in our eyes, our eyes start making a lot of tears. It's the body's way of cleaning things up.

A Little Chemical Factory, Tasty Too!

This is a picture of an onion cell. There are millions of them in an onion and you need a microscope to see them. The little pockets are called vacuoles (vac-U-olz) and they hold a chemical called allinase (AL-in-aze).

When you bump or cut an onion, the allinase mixes with other chemicals in the cell and that makes all kinds of new chemicals. The one that hurts our eyes has a very long name. It is called (Z)-propan-ethial S-oxide. That's what Mr. Block figured out. That chemical turns from liquid into vapor very fast. It turns into fumes. Perfume works the same way. When that happens, it gets in our nose and eyes. Yes, your nose is connected to your eyes!

Vacuole

Nucleus

Cytoplasm

Controlling Things

EXPERIMENT #2

WHAT YOU NEED: An adult - kitchen knife - onion

WHAT TO DO: Share this with a grown-up. They will like knowing how to do this. Put the onion in your refrigerator. Leave it there for 2 hours. Then slice it. Now try slicing it in a sink underwater.*

⚠ Never use a sharp knife without first asking permission!

WHAT IS GOING ON: The stuff that stings our eyes has to turn into a vapor before it can get into our eyes. Cold things do not evaporate as fast as warm things. The onion didn't sting as much when it was cold.

*When you cut up the onion underwater, the fumes got dissolved in the water. Even though water works well, chilling an onion is an easier way to stop your eyes from crying.

Dear Beakman,

How do you make paint?

Cristy

Dear Cristy,

Paints are all just about the same. They all have pigment – which is the color – and a vehicle – the liquid in which the color is carried. Paint started as a way to decorate cave walls with pictures. Now paint is also a protection. The right kind of vehicle in the paint can keep out weather and water. If you make some paint, keep in mind that there will always be someone around to tell you how to use it. These people are called critics (CRIT-icks), and they'd rather tell you how to paint than paint themselves.

Beakman

Beakman

91

You Can Make Some Paint

WHAT YOU NEED: A brick - hammer - old cooking pan - eggs - water - ⚠ safety glasses or sunglasses

WHAT TO DO: Put on the glasses. They'll protect your eyes. Use the hammer to knock off a chunk of the brick's corner. Use a red brick. Smash up the chunk of brick into tiny pieces and put them in the pot. (This isn't very easy. But they say that artists have to suffer. Maybe this is what that means.) Add a little spoonful of water. Now use the handle of the hammer to pound the brick bits till you get a paste. If you're clever, you can talk someone into helping you because this will take time.

MORE STUFF TO DO: For every 2 tablespoons of paste you have, you'll need 1 egg yolk. Ask a grown-up to show you how to separate an egg. Mix up the yolk with a fork till it looks lemony. Now add the paste and stir it up really well. You just made paint. The brick dust is colored red by a chemical called iron oxide (rust). It's the pigment. The egg yolks are the vehicle.

Another Kind of Paint You Can Make

EXPERIMENT #2

WHAT YOU NEED: Colored chalk - white glue - the hammer and pot and glasses from Experiment #1

WHAT TO DO: Instead of pounding on bricks for a long time, try grinding up and pounding on chalk. It's a lot easier. You'll be surprised at the small amount of powder you'll get. There's a lot of air in chalk.

Grind your chalk in a little water like in the first experiment. For every two sticks of chalk you use, add $1/4$ cup water and 1 tablespoon of white glue. Mix it all up really well.

Try mixing different colored chalks. One red stick of chalk and another that's yellow should give you orange paint. Experiment on your own with vehicles and pigments. Soft rocks are good for some colors. The soot from inside a fireplace will give you black. An important part of art is experimenting.

The most expensive paint there is is made from a gemstone. Real ultramarine blue paint is used by artists, but not very often because it costs a lot. It's made by grinding up the gem lapis lazuli – a beautiful blue gem. Most of the ultramarine blue paint sold is imitation.

Dear Beakman,

How do you make pencils?

Mariah

Dear Mariah,

Pencils with erasers let you do something most ink pens won't. They let you make mistakes. *You Can* erase pencil mistakes. Pencil leads aren't really lead. Lead is a toxic metal, and there isn't any lead in a pencil at all. We call it lead because that's how the idea started. In ancient times people used pieces of lead to write with. They didn't know real lead is poison.

Beakman

Beakman

What Is a Pencil Lead?

WHAT YOU NEED: Pencil - paper

WHAT TO DO: Draw a box and fill it in. Make the box as black as you can. Keep coloring it with your pencil until it is shiny. Rub your finger back and forth on the box. Compare how that feels to rubbing on plain paper.

WHAT IS GOING ON: It felt slippery on the black box, and that's a clue. Pencil lead is really graphite (GRAF-eyt), which is a kind of carbon. Graphite molecules are kind of like tiny plates that slip and slide on top of each other.

To make pencil lead, graphite is mixed with clay and squeezed out of a mold – like toothpaste. Then it's baked. The higher the number on your pencil, the more clay there is. Higher numbers are harder pencils. Low numbers are softer. Most of us use a number 2 pencil. Compare the lines different numbered pencils make.

This Pencil Is Softer Than A #3

This Pencil Is Harder Than A #2

95

Drawing on the Past

Pencils are really old. The ancient Greeks and the Aztecs both used real lead to write with. That was thousands of years ago.

In 1770 an English scientist named Joseph Priestley found out that rubber would rub away pencil marks. In fact, that's why he named it rubber.

In 1812 a whole new and better pencil was invented. It didn't use lead, and it could be erased with the new improvement – an eraser stuck on one end. People loved it. For the first time, they could fix mistakes. It's the same kind of pencil we use today.

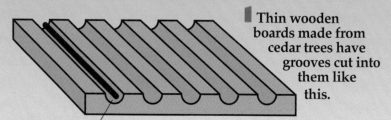

1 Thin wooden boards made from cedar trees have grooves cut into them like this.

2 The core of the pencil – the lead – is laid in the grooves.

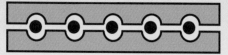

3 Another piece of grooved cedar is laid on top and glued down tight.

4 The pencils are cut apart with a saw. Then they are painted and an eraser is stuck on the end.

Very pure graphite was found in a mine in Ticonderoga, New York (ti-CON-dur-O-gah). You'll see that name on many pencils. Look for it. The company that makes them is named after the Ticonderoga graphite mines.

Dear Beakman,

How does a phonograph record work?

Kenny

Dear Kenny,

The word itself explains a lot about phono-graphs. Phono means *sound*. And graphic means *written*. Phonographic means *written with sound*. A record is covered with grooves written by sounds. Our record players read that sound-writing. Back in olden times, in the 1960s, before cassettes and CDs, records and records on radio were the only ways for music to be shared on a mass scale. Records were so important to culture, words about them became slang words – like groovy. Ask your family and grandparents for other words.

Beakman

Beakman

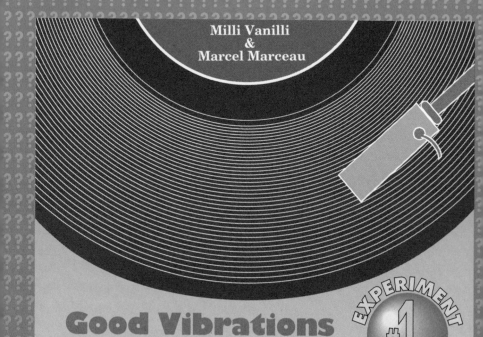

Milli Vanilli
&
Marcel Marceau

Good Vibrations
Get in the Groove

EXPERIMENT #1

WHAT YOU NEED: A plastic soda bottle - scissors - balloon

WHAT TO DO: ⚠ Cut the bottom of the bottle away. Cut the very end of the balloon off, the end you blow up. Now stretch the top of the balloon over the top of the bottle. Pull it down so the balloon is tight. Pick up the bottle and hold the open end right up to your mouth. Hold a finger very lightly on the tight balloon. Start talking or yelling into the bottle.

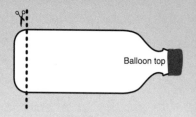

Balloon top

Say the word *vibration* or *groovy*. What's happening at the other end under your finger?

WHAT IS GOING ON: The balloon buzzed under your fingers. It was vibrating. The sound waves from your yelling made the balloon shiver. If you could attach a pencil to the balloon, you would be able to draw a wavy line just with the sound of your voice. The pencil would shiver, too. A record groove is a long wavy line made by a vibrating cutting needle at the record factory. That needle behaves just like the pencil would – it vibrates and writes a wavy line.

Make a Phonograph

EXPERIMENT #2

WHAT YOU NEED: Piece of paper - pin - old phonograph record - turntable from your stereo

WHAT TO DO: Make a cone with the paper. Use some tape to make sure the cone doesn't open at the side. Go outside and lightly scrape the pin on the sidewalk a few times. This will dull the point a bit. Stick it through the end of the cone. This is your record player. In fact, it's a lot like the first phonographs ever made.

Playing a record with a pin will cut away some of the groove and wreck the record. So, find an old record that no one cares about, something like Tony Orlando and Dawn. Don't use a family favorite.

Put the record on the turntable and turn it on. Hold the cone from the large end and gently place the pin on the record. What happened?

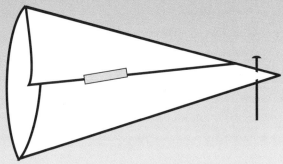

WHAT IS GOING ON: You just made a Victrola – an old-fashioned record player that didn't use electricity. The wavy grooves in your record made the pin vibrate. The cone made the vibrations louder. Those vibrations are the music.

The first phonograph used cylinders, not disks. It was invented by Thomas Alva Edison. The first words ever recorded were Mr. Edison reading "Mary Had a Little Lamb."

Dear Beakman,

Why do electrical plugs always have two prongs?

Mike

Dear Mike,

Electricity is electrons flowing. Plugs have *at least* 2 prongs because electricity must flow in a loop. One prong is for electricity *in*. The other is for electricity *out*.

Electricity is not a thing – not an object. Instead, it is something that occurs like an event or happening. When a happening has a name, we say that it is a phenomenon (fee-NOM-eh-non).

Beakman

Beakman

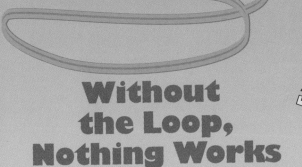

Without the Loop, Nothing Works

EXPERIMENT #1

WHAT YOU NEED: Working flashlight - short piece of wire

WHAT TO DO: Turn on the flashlight to make sure it works. Take it apart so that you have the batteries and the light bulb. Try to make it work without the flashlight case. Put the bulb on top of the battery. Touch them together. Try the bottom. Try 2 batteries at once. You know that the flashlight works. So why won't this work? If you get a little angry, that's called being frustrated (FRUS-tray-ted).Getting the bulb to light can make you very frustrated.

WHAT IS GOING ON:

I did this experiment when I was 8 years old and got so angry I nearly cried. My cousin George helped me understand that we would never get the lightbulb to light just by touching it to the battery.

That's because electricity has to flow through the bulb for it to work. Electricity is electrons flowing.The only way to get the bulb to light is to use the wire to connect the side of the bulb to the bottom of the battery. Then electrons can flow in a loop.

101

Shocking Discoveries
Don't Get In The Loop

Plugs and outlets are dangerous because our bodies conduct electricity. It can flow through our bodies. When that happens, we get shocked and it can kill us.

⚠ *Never mess with an outlet.*

To see and understand the loop safely, use this drawing instead of a real lamp. Start at (**1**) and follow the line up through the bulb, back down to the wire and back into the plug.

Pretend you're electricity. Use a pencil to follow the line. The only way the bulb – or any other appliance – will work is if you end up at number (**2**).

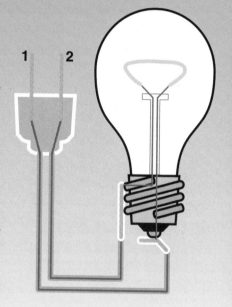

The loop is completed back at the electric company. There, a big machine called a generator uses magnets to pump electrons through the wires.

As long as we don't become a part of that loop, we won't get shocked. To stay out of the loop, don't ever touch any part of it.

The third prong on some plugs is called a ground. In some countries it's called the earth. The ground wire is designed to carry electricity into the Earth if a short circuit happens. The idea is to keep us from getting shocked.

Dear Beakman,

Why does popcorn pop?

Marlo

Dear Marlo,

Popcorn is really a kind of grass seed that gets really steamed up and explodes. All kinds of corn are really kinds of grass. Popcorn is a very hard kernel that is sealed tight. Inside it's damp. When the moisture reaches 400 degrees, it turns into super-heated steam and explodes the kernel. The white fluffy popcorn we all love is the insides of the seed – cooked by the steam and turned inside out by the explosion.

Beakman

Beakman

Popcorn that Pops - or Popcorn Duds

WHAT YOU NEED: Popcorn - hammer - help from a grown-up - pan with lid and a bit of cooking oil

WHAT TO DO: Spread some popcorn out on some concrete, like a garage or basement floor. Use the hammer to crack each kernel into pieces. Give them to your grown-up to pop. Grown-ups will usually help you if you say you're doing an experiment. Don't mention that the corn won't pop. The secret is, you turned all the kernels into duds. They won't pop. Make your helper guess why.

WHAT IS GOING ON: Popcorn pops because about 13% of the kernel inside is water. When the water is heated inside the sealed seed, pressure builds up and the kernel pops open as steam is released. When you cracked the kernels, you broke the seal. Pressure couldn't build up to pop the corn. The duds in regular uncracked popcorn are either too dry inside or have little cracks in their shells.

Popcorn makes a great replacement for those plastic foam pellets people use in boxes. In other popcorn news, cornstarch from unpopped popcorn may one day be made into plastic bags that can decompose when we're through using them.

Home Grown
Each Kernel Can Make a Whole Stalk of Corn

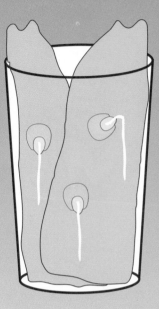

Line a glass with a paper towel. Then wad up several more paper towels and stick them inside. Now place a couple popcorn kernels in between the glass and the toweling. Gently add water until the towels soak it up. Keep it wet for 4-5 days. A little root will come out and will always point down, no matter which way the seed points. If you plant it in soil, your corn will be 5 feet tall in a few months.

Dear Beakman,

How does radio work?

Melanie

Dear Melanie,

Radios pick up radio waves, which begin at radio station towers. The waves are pulses of electromagnetism, and they can carry music, talking or computer data. Even television is really radio. TV pictures are sent into our homes on radio waves. *You Can* do these experiments to understand better.

Beakman

Beakman

How Waves Move

WHAT YOU NEED: Bathtub of water
- a few pennies - a wooden toothpick

WHAT TO DO: At bath time, fill the
tub but don't put anything in it. Wait until the water is smooth.
Drop a penny in it and watch the ripples. Now float the toothpick
in one end and drop a penny in the other end. Watch the toothpick as the ripple goes by. Take out all the stuff you dropped in
and take your bath.

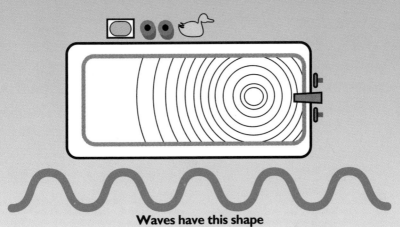

Waves have this shape

WHAT IS GOING ON:

Sound, light and magnetism all move in waves. Your penny
started waves. When a wave goes by, it does not move the water
with it. The wave moves through the water. That's why your
toothpick stayed in the same place, bobbing up and down. Radio
is electromagnetism moving in waves through space. We can
change the height or the number of waves quickly. That's how we
put information in them. FM radio changes the number of waves.
AM radio changes the height of the wave.

You Can build a real radio yourself. Really. A crystal radio is very simple
but it works great. A kit to build one costs about $8. A store called
Radio Shack sells them.

Radio Stations in Your House

WHAT YOU NEED: AM radio - household appliances - permission from your family to use the appliances

WHAT TO DO: Tune the radio until it is not on a radio station – until you hear noise. Turn up the volume. Turn on one or more of the following things: vacuum cleaner, blender, electric razor, hair dryer, fan, food processor. Listen to the radio.

WHAT IS GOING ON: Those appliances have motors, and all electric motors work with electromagnetism and give off electromagnetic waves, or radio. Your radio picks them up and turns them into sound. If you have a code, you can even send messages to a friend using a vacuum cleaner. *You Can* find the Morse Code in your library.

Vacuum cleaner or radio station?

Almost 100 Years Old

Guglielmo Marconi with his radio in 1895

Radio is one of the first inventions that put together lots of other inventions and other ideas. When that happens today, we say that it is a system. In 1895 a scientist in Italy named Guglielmo Marconi (goo-li-EL-mo mar-CON-ee) built the first successful radio. Many people, including inventor Nikola Tesla and physicist Heinrich Hertz, were working on it because scientists thought that it might be possible. When that happens we say there was a theory (THEAR-ee). It was a kind of guess that radio was possible. Marconi's first radio couldn't transmit music – just a lot of clicks. The clicks could send messages using Morse Code.

Dear Beakman,

I like your comic and I have a question. How do they recycle paper?

Patrick

Dear Patrick,

Paper is made from cellulose (SELL-u-los), which is in plant fibers. The cellulose is made by grinding up trees. Recycling uses cellulose over and over again. Recycled paper can be made with less electricity, with less water, with a lot less pollution and it saves trees from being cut down. *You Can* use this procedure to make recycled paper at home.

Beakman

Beakman

Recycled Paper Procedure
Follow this Step by Step

First, some information: Making recycled paper is messy. It is also a lot of fun. Someone will have to use a food processor and an electric iron. Both can be dangerous. So make sure that you get help on this project because it is a big one. It is best to do this with some friends and family. That way you can spread the mess and the fun around.

WHAT YOU NEED: 2 full newspaper pages torn into 2 inch squares - food processor - 2 tablespoons white glue - 2 or 3 cups water - sink with 4 inches water - old panty hose - coat hangers - electric iron. *OPTIONAL: insect screen - strainer - food coloring*

Step #1

Undo the coat hanger and use the wire to make a flat square about 6 by 8 inches big. Stretch one leg of the panty hose over it. Take your time; it could snag. If you put tape on the ends of the wire, it will snag less. Make sure it is tight and flat. Tie knots in the hose. Use the other leg for another piece of paper. You will need one frame for every piece of paper you make. You might want to make more than one or two.

Make your frame like this

Don't get fooled. When a bag or a box says that it is 100% recyclable that means that you can recycle it. It does not mean that it is made out of recycled paper.

Step #2

Put a handful of the paper and some water into the food processor. ⚠ Close the food processor and turn it on high. Keep adding paper and water until you have a big gray blob. You may have to add a little more water to keep things moving smoothly. Keep the food processor on until all the paper has disappeared. Then leave it on for 2 whole minutes. Put the glue in the sink water and add all of the paper pulp you just made. Mix it real good. Use your hands.

The ink in the newpaper makes the paper pulp look like a blob of gross gray gunk.

Mix up the sink water again and then scoop the frame to the bottom of the sink. Lift it real slow. Count to 20 slowly while you are lifting. Let the water drain out for about a minute. Mix up the sink every time you make a new piece.

Step #3

Try other things like the screen or a strainer. Try adding about one half teaspoon of food coloring to the water.

Now you have to hang the frames on a clothesline or put them out in the sun. Wait until they are completely dry with no dampness at all. *You Can* then gently peel off the paper. Have a grown-up use the iron - set on the hottest setting - to steam out your paper. *You Can* keep making paper until the pulp is all strained out of the sink.

See how strong your paper is. Trim it with scissors. Write on it. It is strong. If there is a microscope at school, use it to look at the fibers in your paper. Compare it to newspaper.

111

Dear Beakman,

I wonder how satellites work. Can you tell me how? Thanks.

Matt

Dear Matt,

When people use the word "satellite" it is often an adjective – like in *satellite TV*. But a satellite is really any star, planet, moon or asteroid that orbits another larger celestial body. The Earth is one of the Sun's satellites. The Moon is the Earth's natural satellite. The ones that we *call* satellites are really artificial satellites. *You Can* do these 2 experiments to learn how a communications satellite works.

Beakman

Beakman

What Keeps Them Up There?

WHAT YOU NEED: Piece of string - short piece of crayon

WHAT TO DO: Wrap one end of the string around the middle of the crayon. Tie a knot to hold it tight. Hold the other end of the string and spin the string around and around over your head. ⚠ (Do this outside and don't hit anyone else.)

WHAT IS GOING ON: The crayon pulled the string tight and moved in a blurred circle over your head. The string acts like the Earth's gravity, which is a kind of pull. It keeps satellites from flying off into space. Your string kept the crayon from flying away just like gravity. Simple, isn't it? The pull of gravity also keeps the Moon in orbit and keeps you and me on the Earth.

Satellites work in a similar way. Gravity is always pulling them down towards Earth. But they go so fast that when they fall it is not down to the ground, it's down around Earth. A little confusing? Perhaps. When a satellite is in orbit, it is not really flying. It is falling around and falling around the Earth.

In most libraires books on satellites have the number 629.4 Check it out!

113

Satellites Are Like Mirrors

EXPERIMENT #2

WHAT YOU NEED: Flashlight - mirror - a friend - two rooms with a wall in between

WHAT TO DO: Stand in one room and try to get your flashlight to shine in the other where your friend is. If you can't figure out how to do it, look at the diagram. The red bar is a mirror. The dotted lines are light from your flashlight.

WHAT IS GOING ON: A satellite picks up radio waves. It then sends them back to Earth.

SO WHAT: Microwave radio is like light. It can go only in straight lines. But the Earth is round. For straight lines of radio waves to go from one side of Earth to the other, they need the help of a satellite. It works just like the mirror.

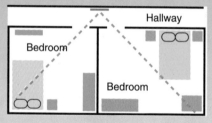

Hallway

Bedroom

Bedroom

Satellite TV

The World's First Communications Satellite

This is a picture of Telstar, the world's first communications satellite. It was launched in 1962. Telstar was built by AT&T, a phone company sometimes called Ma Bell. The satellite was so popular a band called The Tornadoes made a rock 'n' roll song called "Telstar" that was a big hit. Like all communications satellites since, Telstar worked by picking up a radio signal from one part of the Earth and broadcasting it back down to another part of the world. Without these satellites we couldn't get live TV from across oceans.

Dear Beakman,

How can you make fake slime like in the Ghostbuster movies?

Howie

Dear Howie,

You Can get movie slime from places called theatrical supply houses. In some cities they are in the Yellow Pages. *You Can* make an excellent slime at home after a trip to the drug store. *You Can* also make fake blood and some make-up at home. Make-up is safer than masks. But it can be a big mess. Make sure your family says it's OK.

Beakman

Beakman

Movie
Make-up

BEARDS

Ask a grown-up to touch the end of a cork to a candle flame. ⚠ After it burns a bit, then cools off, you can use it like a crayon to give yourself a beard. *You Can* dress up like Bruce Willis, a movie star who doesn't shave very well. When the cork burned you freed the carbon in the cork. That's what is black. You'll have to wash well to get rid of your beard.

CLOWN WHITE

You Can make a paste that will turn your face and hands white by mixing a lot of cornstarch with a very little bit of cooking oil. Use a fork to mix it. It will take some time.

FAKE BLOOD

It's too bad that there is a lot of this stuff in movies. One make-up artist makes it by mixing light corn syrup with red and yellow food coloring. Apply it with a dropper. Don't make a mess. It will be dark red and shiny.

Fake Slime

WHAT YOU NEED:
Tube or jar of clear hair setting gel (from drug store) - food coloring - water - your family's permission

WHAT TO DO: Squeeze out all of the gel into a small bowl. Add three or four drops of water. Add one or two drops of food coloring. Mix. If it's too thick, add a few drops of water. Your slime will be a gooey, drippy mess. This tends to upset families, so be careful not to spill it. The food color can stain clothes and carpets. If you don't put the food color in, your slime will not stain. Do not use this on your face. The gel might sting your eyes. *You Can* make another kind of slime by boiling cornstarch and water. It's a lot like gravy. Add some food coloring and let it cool and you can use this on your face.

Slime
Sometimes It's Real

Whole families of molds live as a big slimy mess. Molds are the fuzzy things growing on old food in the back of the refrigerator. Slime molds actually crawl around. They're creepy but some people keep them as a kind of pet.

You Can see pictures of real slime mold in the July 1991 issue of Smithsonian Magazine. It is horrible looking. Ask the librarian at your library to help you find a copy.

117

Dear Beakman,

Can you tell me how soap works? I have to use it all the time. Mom says it's magic, but I don't think so.

Katie

Dear Katie,

Soap works by making water wetter than it already is. Really! Soap can also mix with both oil or grease and water at the same time! *You Can* do these two experiments to see how soap works.

Beakman

Beakman

What? Wetter Water?

You Can tell how wet water is by looking at a kind of skin it makes. It's called the surface tension. If that skin is not broken, nothing gets wet.

WHAT YOU NEED: Clear drinking glass - teaspoon - liquid dish soap

WHAT TO DO: Fill the glass with water. Look close at the edge. Use the teaspoon to add more water. *You Can* add more than you think. Add it until you see the water come up out of the glass. This shows you the surface tension. Add a drop of dish soap near the edge of the glass. Be sure to be looking at the surface tension when you do it. What happened?

WHAT IS GOING ON:
When you add soap to water the water gets thinner than it already is. That is why the water ran down the side of the glass when you added the soap. The wetter water can now wet things that would not break the surface tension of regular water.

WHAT YOU NEED: Jar with lid - water - cooking oil - liquid dish soap

WHAT TO DO: Fill the jar half full of water. Then add four tablespoons of cooking oil. Close the lid tight. Shake it as hard as you can. The oil and water will NOT MIX. No matter how hard you shake the jar they will always separate. Now add a teaspoon full of dish soap. Close the jar and shake it again. Real hard. What happened?

WHAT IS GOING ON: The smallest bits of soap possible are called molecules (MOL-ee-kuuls). They are very very tiny. A soap

Oil and water will not mix. No matter how hard you try.

Add soap and things change.

molecule can hook onto a water molecule. It can also hook onto an oil molecule. When greasy dirt is grabbed by a soap molecule and a water molecule you can rinse it away with more water. It is called emulsify. The soap emulsified (ee-MUL-sah-fied) the oil and the water turned gray. To save water when there isn't any rain, people can use gray water from sinks and showers to water plants.

⚠ *But, do not drink it!*

Do not throw your experiment down the drain! The water is still good for plants and trees. Go outside and give the gray water to a plant. They need it!

Dear Beakman,

Why does soda fizz? How does that happen?

Chris

Dear Chris,

Soda is one of those things that shows how really big the United States and Canada are. They are so big, people who live in different parts of them call the same thing by completely different names. In a lot of places it's called pop. In others, it's soda. To make sure everybody understands, I'll call it soda pop. Soda pop is carbonated (KAR-bun-a-ted), which means a gas has been dissolved in it.

That's what fizzes.

Beakman

Beakman

Something You Do Every Day

WHAT YOU NEED: A kitchen faucet - a drinking glass.

WHAT TO DO: Make sure the faucet has an aerator on the end. Most do. Many have a ring of holes around the end. It lets in the air. Turn on the faucet full blast. Stick the glass under it. Then look at the water in the glass. You'll see bubbles. They don't last long. If your faucet has an air ring, cover it and turn on the faucet. (Or remove the aerator.) The water will be flat and won't bubble.

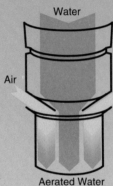

Water

Air

Aerated Water

WHAT IS GOING ON: You just dissolved gases in water. The gases are air. Most of them bubbled out very quickly. But if you put that water glass beside your bed at night, in the morning you'll see little bubbles again. They are full of the air you dissolved in the water. Air will mix with water. But we can't mix enough of it to make the water fizz. The gas that makes soda pop fizz mixes better with water. For every amount of air we can mix in, we could have mixed in 26 times as much carbon dioxide.

There is carbon dioxide in the air. In fact, every time we blow out a breath there's carbon dioxide in it. That's because our bodies make carbon dioxide.

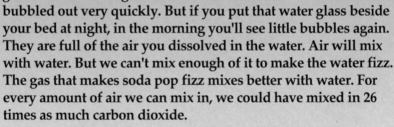

Soda Pop
Fizzed & Fizzled

In 1772, a chemist in England named Joseph Priestley was trying to find a way of making mineral water. Health resorts in Europe were serving this fizzy water and saying that it was a kind of cure for illnesses. It was very popular. And people were making lots of money serving it. Some people even bathed in it. It came from water springs in only one area of France. It came up out of the ground fizzing and no one knew what made it fizz.

Priestley mixed minerals with water and it didn't fizz. He then mixed a gas with the water. The gas was carbon dioxide (KAR-bun di-OX-ide). It fizzed. But it fizzled as a product. That is, it was a flop as a drink. It took until 1850 before people started buying flavored and sweetened sparkling water – soda pop. Priestley did make an important discovery, though. He found out you can dissolve a gas in a liquid.

We all know you can dissolve a solid, like sugar, in a liquid like water. But no one knew you could dissolve a gas in water before Priestley did it.

Shake It Up, Baby

EXPERIMENT #2

WHAT YOU NEED: A large bottle of soda pop (the clear plastic kind) - ice - permission from your family

WHAT TO DO: Don't open the bottle just yet. Shake it up as hard as you can. The soda pop will fizz and then stop fizzing. Keep shaking. Each time, there will be less fizzing and it will stop. Now open the bottle carefully. Don't make a mess. Look closely at the bottle. Where do the fizz bubbles start? Pour a glass for yourself. Did it fizz? Add ice. What happened?

WHAT IS GOING ON:
When you shook the bottle you were forcing the carbon dioxide out of solution. It was mixed with the water in the soda pop. You forced it out. Then it built up in the little air space at the top of the bottle. There was so much pressure no more carbon dioxide could get out of the water and into the air. That's why it stopped fizzing. It started again when you opened the bottle and released the pressure. The bubbles form on little imperfections in the plastic. The plastic is not fizzing. Ice has lots of imperfections – nooks and crannies– which is why the soda pop fizzed even more when you put in ice cubes.

Dear Beakman,

Why do the stars come out only at night?

Jason

Dear Jason,

The stars are always there. We just can't see them. We can't because the light from our nearest star is so bright, it overpowers light from the other stars. The star nearest to Earth is our sun. We can see the other stars only when it's night and the light from the sun is blocked by the Earth.

You Can make a model of the sky to see how this works.

Beakman

Beakman

Orion

(o-RI-an)
The Hunter

In ancient times, people tried to make sense of the sky. They played connect the dots with the stars. Orion is one group of stars. The groups are called constellations (kan-stel-LA-shenz). He is just imaginary and isn't really up in the sky. You can see Orion best in the winter months of January and February in the Southern sky. Look south at around 9 p.m. To find south, remember where the sun sets. Look that direction. Toward your left will be south. Look that way to see Orion.

Constellations are a part of something called astrology (ah-STRAHL-o-gee), which is a kind of fortune telling. Astrology uses lots of math and measuring, but it is not a science. Instead, astrology is an art, and no one can prove if it works or not.

Build a Star Box

WHAT YOU NEED: Shoe box - paste - scissors - pin - paper - pencil

WHAT TO DO: Trace or copy the picture of Orion on page 125. Paste it down tight inside one end of the shoe box. Cut a hole in the other end so that you can look inside. Cut a flap in the lid. Carefully, stick the pin through all the black dots in the drawing. Make the pinholes for the bigger dots a bit bigger. Put on the lid with the top flap open. Look in the eye hole and slowly close the flap. You'll see the stars come out.

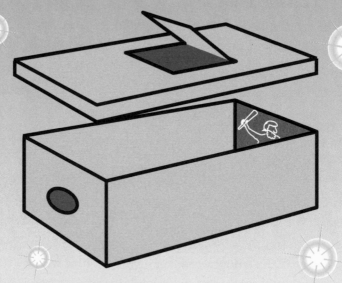

WHAT IS GOING ON:
Light from the stars and from the little holes in the box is not as bright as sunlight. When the sun sets – or when the flap closes – the sky is darker, and we can see the weak light from the stars. At night, stars are brighter than the black sky, so we can see them.

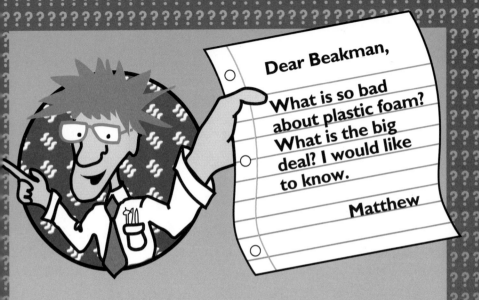

Dear Beakman,

What is so bad about plastic foam? What is the big deal? I would like to know.

Matthew

Dear Matthew,

Plastic foam is controversial (con-trah-VUR-shul). That means different people think different things about it and talk about it a lot. People have to listen to many different sides and make up their own minds whether something is good or bad.

Here are two experiments *You Can* use to help you make up your own mind. And, thanks for writing!

Beakman

Beakman

One of the Things That's Bad

WHAT YOU NEED: Egg beater - measuring cup - spoon - dirty dishes - dish soap.

WHAT TO DO: Fill the sink with water and add dish soap. Use the egg beater to make big piles of suds. Crank it fast and a lot. Use the spoon to fill the cup with suds. Make sure it is just suds and no water at all. Put the cup on a shelf and don't touch it for 6 hours. Do the dishes. Go back 6 hours later and look at the measuring cup. Measure what's left.

WHAT IS GOING ON: Foam is mostly air. 2 cups of suds are made from only 1 tablespoon of water. Plastic foam is like that, too. For 1 spoonful of plastic, we get 10 spoonfuls of plastic foam. Soap bubbles break and turn back to soapy water. Plastic foam does not. It stays the way you see it for hundreds of years. The problem is that means we have to find 10 times as much space to dump it when we're done using it. Think about that. When you take out the trash, think about having to take it out 10 times instead of 1. You'll also need a garbage can that is 10 times as big!

One of the Things That's Good

WHAT YOU NEED: 8 unbroken ice cubes - salad plate - foam burger box (or a foam coffee cup)

WHAT TO DO: Put 4 ice cubes on the plate and put 4 inside the plastic foam burger box. Close the lid of the box and look at the clock. Put both the plate and box in the sunshine and look at them every half hour until the ice on the plate is melted. Then open the box. What is inside?

WHAT IS GOING ON: There was ice in the burger box when the other ice had melted. Plastic foam has millions of bubbles inside and that makes it a great insulator. Hot things stay hot and cold things stay cold. Also the foam box does not get wet and soggy when something melts or drips on it. The bubbles in the foam make it very lightweight. That means it can be put in trucks and shipped using less gasoline.

SO WHAT: Good or bad isn't always an easy question. There are more things to find out about plastic foam. Lots more. Talk to your family about this and decide together. And, decide what to do about it too.

Plastic foam floats! That's good because we can use it in boats, lifesaving rings and floating boat docks. That's bad because fish and turtles think the little pieces of it are food and it can kill them.

Dear Beakman,

Why doesn't food taste good when you have a cold?

Rebecca

Dear Rebecca,

To talk about this subject, we have to use a word that isn't polite. We'll use it anyway so that everyone knows what is being discussed. The word is snot. The polite way of saying it is mucus (MUKE-us). But even that word can be used impolitely. Polite or impolite is more a matter of your intentions.

Snot is thick and sticks to just about everything. It's a good thing, too, because mucus is a barrier against germs. It helps keep them outside. It also cuts off a very important part of the way we taste food.

Beakman

Beakman

Tastes and Smells

EXPERIMENT #1

WHAT YOU NEED: A sugar bowl

WHAT TO DO: Wet your fingertip and dab it into the sugar. Stick your tongue way out and touch the sugar on the very back of your tongue. Don't close your mouth. With your tongue still out, try to taste the sugar. Now touch the sugar to the tip of your tongue.

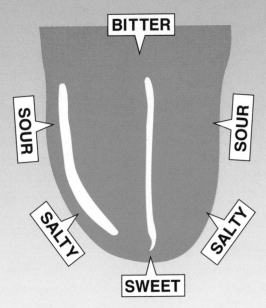

WHAT IS GOING ON: You can't taste sweet on the back of your tongue. Your tongue can taste only 4 different flavors and does it on different parts. We need our sense of smell to give food its full flavor.

You do Experiment #1 every time you lick an ice cream cone. You taste the sweet as you lick the ice cream with the tip of your tongue. The other flavors come from our sense of smell.

The Nose Knows

WHAT YOU NEED: 3 different flavors of a drink mix like Kool-Aid™ - a friend - a blindfold - 4 glasses

WHAT TO DO: Follow the directions on the drink mixes and make all 3 separately. (A lot of people don't buy these drink mixes; but they work real well for this experiment.) Blindfold your friend and pour out a glass of each flavor. In the fourth glass, put a little of each flavor and mix them up. Make sure your friend's nose is held shut tightly. Switch the glasses around and have a taste test. Then you try it. Make sure to hold your nose while you're tasting the drink. What happened?

WHAT IS GOING ON:

When you have a cold, your body is working overtime trying to keep out germs. Several openings in our bodies are protected by mucus. It's a barrier that keeps all that stuff outside. Germs get stuck in the sticky gunk. The problem is we can't smell because our nose is full of snot. That means we can't taste very many flavors. When you held your nose, your drinks had only one taste – sweet. And if you think about it, these drinks don't really taste like what they're called anyway. No real grape tastes anything like a grape drink.

Dear Beakman,

How do they measure tall things? I want to measure the trees in my yard.

Kurt

Dear Kurt,

You need a special kind of math called geometry (gee-AHM-a-tree). It's a very old word that means *measure the Earth*. I know that sometimes math seems like a tremendous drag. But there is really a lot of power and magic in math – and none of it is pretend. The power to answer your own questions frees you to move on to the next challenge. And that is the magic. A lot of people don't have that power and get trapped. *You Can* use today's experiment to start – to measure those trees. Finish it by understanding how it works. Do that by asking your teacher until it makes sense.

Beakman

Beakman

Your Tree Measurer

Before you do Experiment #1, make yourself the tool you'll need. Trace "My Tree Measurer" onto a piece of paper, then paste it to a piece of cardboard. A cereal box is perfect. After the paste is dry, cut along the dotted line. Make sure to keep the shape exactly the way it is now. Follow the dotted line. Punch a hole at the top and stick in a 1-foot piece of string. Tie a big knot in the string so that it won't slip out. Tie a weight – like a screw or washer – on the other end. This tool, plus a tape measure and a friend, is all you need.

You Can use the tool you made to measure how tall houses are, or even skyscrapers. The secret is the triangle's special shape. It has a 90-degree angle and two sides that are the same length. Ask your teacher to explain why that's special.

My Tree Measurer

Punch out hole for string.

Tilt card back and forth until the string lines up with this mark.

YOU
U
CAN

Using Geometry in the Backyard

EXPERIMENT #1

WHAT YOU NEED: Tree measurer - a friend - tape measure

WHAT TO DO: Hold your tree measurer so that the string meets the big dotted line. This means your tool is level and not tilted. Hold it up to your face so that you can look along the top slanted side. Walk toward or away from the tree until *You Can* see the tree top at the end of your sight line. Now stand still a minute. Ask your friend to measure from the star on the tool to the ground using the tape measure. Now your friend should measure from the star to the tree. Add those two together, and that's the height of the tree!

WHAT IS GOING ON:
As long as you and the tree are on flat ground, your tree measurer will work. It works by using a rule about triangles that your teacher can explain to you. Take this to school and ask.

Look along this line.

< The 2 lines are the same length. >

Dear Beakman,

I am interested in how a TV works.

Jonathan

Dear Jonathan,

A television draws a picture line by line and does it very fast. Your brain puts many pictures together and they seem to move. Here are three experiments *You Can* do to understand TV better – at least how it moves.

Beakman

Drawing a Picture Line by Line

EXPERIMENT #1

WHAT YOU NEED: Scissors - white paper - paste - crayons - tape

WHAT TO DO: Cut out a picture from the Sunday comics and paste it to the paper. Turn it over and draw two colored lines on the back. Cut the picture into very skinny strips. Mix them up and look at each one. Now put the picture back together again. The colored lines on the back will help you put the picture back together in the right order. Use the tape to stick them back together before turning the picture over again.

WHAT IS GOING ON: You just did the same thing a TV does. A TV camera takes a picture and then cuts it up into 525 slices. By themselves those lines do not look like much at all. A TV set puts them back together just like you did with the tape. The picture then makes sense again. A TV set does this 30 times every second. That speed is what makes the picture seem to move.

You Actually Need a Brain to Watch TV!

EXPERIMENT #2

WHAT YOU NEED: Phone book - pencil

WHAT TO DO: Look at picture #1 and draw it at the bottom of the first page of your phone book. The picture is sometimes called a stickman. If you like, call it a stickperson. Then draw #2 on the bottom of the next page, but move it over just a tiny bit. Go to the next page and draw #1, moving him or her over a bit more. Go to the next page and draw #2 again. Keep going till you have drawn 40 or 50 stickpeople. Now grab the book and flip the pages with your thumb.

1   2

137

WHAT IS GOING ON: The little guy or girl walked across the bottom of your phone book, right? Well, not really; it just seemed to. We got confused by all the different pictures changing so quick that our brain just puts them all together. We call that an illusion (ee-LU-shun). When something on TV seems to move, it is only because we are looking at lots of different still pictures at a high speed. If you have a videotape deck that has a feature called *frame advance*, you can look at each picture by itself. Try it.

A Clue From TV Light

EXPERIMENT #3

WHAT YOU NEED: Pencil - TV

WHAT TO DO: Wave a pencil back and forth as fast as you can. Do it in front of a window. Look carefully at it. Now turn on the TV and do the same thing about 12 inches from the screen. What's different?

WHAT IS GOING ON: When you waved the pencil in front of a window you saw a blur. The pencil was moving too fast to see. But when you did it in front of a TV you saw five or six pencils, and they seemed to bend. That's a clue about the TV changing pictures very fast. Every time the TV changes a picture, the light blinks. It's so fast we can't see it. Your pencil got lit up by the TV every time the picture blinked. That's why you saw many pencils. There was 1 pencil for every different picture the TV showed you.

The little persons walking throughout this book demonstrate how TV and film work. Grab this book by the lower left hand corner and flip the pages.

Dear Beakman,

How can you watch one TV channel while you videotape another channel? We even have cable and can't do it.

Glenn

Dear Glenn,

When you do something step by step, that is called a procedure (pro-SEE-duhr). Here is a procedure *You Can* use to see if your TV and VCR are hooked up right.

Beakman

Beakman

Why It Does Not Work
(Chart-A)

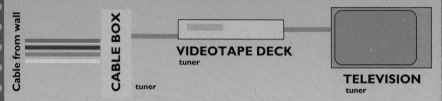

Your cable box and your VCR and your TV all have tuners. A tuner is like a CHOOSER for channels. All the channels come into your house from the cable. The cable box will choose one channel only. Here it's the green channel.

Because your VCR is receiving just the green channel, the VCR's tuner (chooser) cannot choose another channel for you to watch while the VCR tapes the green channel. The cable box stopped the others because it can only choose one channel at a time.

You Can Make It Work Like This
(Chart-B)

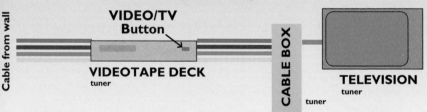

Your VCR can choose a channel to tape without stopping the other channels from going to your TV. The VCR's tuner chooses the channel it will tape. The VIDEO/TV switch lets YOU choose. You can choose to watch VIDEO (what the VCR's tuner has chosen) or you can choose TV - which is any other channel on your cable box.

You can watch one channel on the cable box's chooser while the VCR tapes a channel from its chooser. Your VCR must have a cable-ready tuner. If not, you can record only from cable-channels 2-13. To watch a tape, select channel 3 or 4 on your cable box.

▮▮ OR ●● **All the colors on your TV are made from just these three colors! Look real close and you can see them. Don't look too long. It is not good for your eyes!**

VCR Procedure
Remember: Follow this step by step

1 Get a grown-up to help you. They will think they taught you something and that makes them feel good. Really you teach each other. But that is a secret. It is also safer to have a grown-up there and they bought the VCR so will want to be there. Get a grown-up!

2 Ask the grown-up to disconnect the power from the TV, the VCR and the cable box.

3 With your grown-up, follow the TV cable from the wall to see which comes first - the cable box or the VCR.

4 If your cable looks like Chart-A the two of you have to change it to look like Chart-B.

5 Grown-ups sometimes think things are harder to do than they really are. Stay there and help them by looking at the charts. Tell them you "know they can do it!"

6 When you get things all set up right, turn things on and try the VIDEO/TV switch. It lets YOU choose whether to watch the VCR's tuner or the cable box's tuner.

If you get any pay channels you will not be able to tape them. The cable box must choose pay channels. But you can watch a pay channel while you tape a free channel!

Dear Beakman,

Which way is down?

Jason

Dear Jason,

The answer depends on where you are. That's because the Earth is nearly spherical. A sphere (SFEAR) is like a ball. The way down in Minnetonka, Minnesota, is the way up off the western coast of Australia. And there is a special place where the rules change. At the exact center of the planet, every direction is straight up. Confused? *You Can* do these experiments to clear things up.

Beakman

Beakman

Thinking Globally

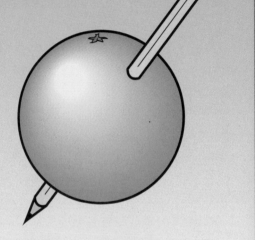

EXPERIMENT #1

WHAT YOU NEED: Pencil - orange

WHAT TO DO: Think of the stem as the North Pole of the Earth. Ask someone to show you where on the planet you live. Or look at a globe. Stick the pencil in the orange at that place and aim for the center. That's the way down from where you live. Keep pushing and see where it comes out. Take out the pencil and drop the orange on the floor.

WHAT IS GOING ON: Even though it looks flat, the Earth is shaped like a ball – or an orange. That means there is an infinite number of ways down. When you dropped the orange, it went down – straight toward the center of the Earth. But that direction was only for you and the place you're at.

Down is a different direction for every spot on Earth. To demonstrate that the Earth is like a ball, just look at the view. You can't see past the horizon. That's because the Earth is curving down away from your point of view. If the Earth was flat, you could see from Minnesota to Australia.

Looking Locally

WHAT YOU NEED:
The orange from Experiment #1

WHAT TO DO: Ask someone who knows about knives to slice the orange in half. ⚠ (Do not do this yourself if you're not allowed to use a kitchen knife. They can be dangerous.) Look inside and use your powers of imagination. Think of the skin as the surface of Earth. Put yourself on a spot. Ask yourself, which way is down? The answer is the direction that's toward the center of the orange. Now put yourself on a different part of the orange. Did the way down change? Imagine you're at the center of the orange. Every way toward the skin would be the way up.

If you're here, the way down is like this:

Both arrows point toward the way down.

But if you're here, the way down is different.

If you think this is strange, it gets more weird when you think about the universe. On the planet Mars, down is toward the center of that planet – not toward our planet's center. In outer space, where there is no gravity, there is no down and no up at all.

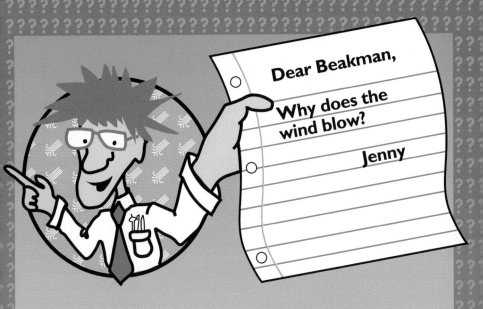

Dear Beakman,

Why does the wind blow?

Jenny

Dear Jenny,

Nature likes things balanced. That goes for heat, too. It tries to balance temperatures. The wind blows because the Earth is not heated evenly by the sun. The air moves up and down because of heat and cold. When that happens, more air rushes in to take its place. That is wind. Because the Earth is round and because it spins, the sun's heat will never be even. So the wind will keep on blowing.

Beakman

Beakman

145

Uneven Heating

WHAT YOU NEED: Flashlight - dark room

WHAT TO DO: Hold the light straight toward the wall and turn it on. Now tilt the light so that it's shining on the wall near the ceiling. Notice how the light spreads out.

WHAT IS GOING ON: You just made a model of the Earth and sun. Because the world is ball-shaped – or spherical (SFIR-i-kel) – the light spreads out at the North and South Poles. It's stronger at the middle, which is called the equator. This is why it's hot at the equator and cold at the North and South Poles.

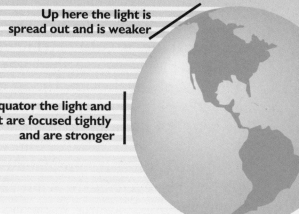

Up here the light is spread out and is weaker

At the Equator the light and heat are focused tightly and are stronger

Warm Things Go Up
Cold Things Go Down

WHAT YOU NEED: Candle - a grown-up - food coloring - water - ice cube tray

EXPERIMENT #2

WHAT TO DO: Fill the ice cube tray with water and add 4 drops of red or green coloring to two cubes. When they're frozen solid, gently place 1 cube into a clear glass of water. Let the water get calm first. Look quickly and closely. The second cube is a spare. It helps to have a light on behind the glass. ⚠ Have the grown-up light the candle. You blow it out. Watch where the smoke goes.

WHAT IS GOING ON: The smoke rose up into the air because it's warmer than the rest of the air. As it rose, it also cooled. When the temperatures were balanced, the smoke stopped going up and just spread out.

The colored ice cube gave off swirls of color like the drawing, and they sank to the bottom of the glass. The colored water was colder than the clear water, so it flowed down. Hot and cold air behave the same – hot air goes up, cold air goes down.

So What:
You Don't Need a Weatherman to Know Which Way the Wind Blows.*

Air rising and falling is much bigger and more powerful than your experiment, and it's what drives all the wind. Hot air at the equator lifts up from the ground like your smoke. When it does, something has to take the place of the air that just went up. Cold air from the North and South Poles is sucked down toward the equator. This causes enormous winds. It all has to do with uneven heating by the sun. That means that all wind and power from wind mills started with the energy in the sun.

*This is a line from a song written a long time ago by a man named Bob Dylan. What it means is sometimes we can figure things out for ourselves – that we don't need experts as often as we think we do.

Dear Beakman,

When will the world come to an end? Please explain.

Matthew

Dear Matthew,

That is a very heavy question! The answer depends on your point of view. For example, if you were a dinosaur, the world has already come to an end. There have been several major extinctions on Earth since life first began. But these happened over millions of years, and some form of life survived and grew. The end of planet Earth itself is in the far future – not for 5 or 6 billion years. So there's plenty of time for you and your friends to celebrate life.

Beakman

Beakman

How Much Is 6 Billion?

WHAT YOU NEED: A paper and pencil
Optional: Calculator

WHAT TO DO: Start with the number 6 billion. It's a 6 followed by 9 zeros. Divide it by the longest number of years you think someone can live. The answer is the number of lifetimes until the sun runs out of hydrogen.

This is the answer I got – 60,000,000. Six billion years is 60 million lifetimes if people live to be 100 years old. So you see, 6 billion is a very big number. The only time it seems small is when politicians start talking about money. But they're wrong. Six billion of anything is an awful lot.

$$\begin{array}{r} 60{,}000{,}000 \\ 100\overline{)6{,}000{,}000{,}000} \end{array}$$

Our Sun
The Source of Our Energy

If you look at every source of energy we have on Earth, you'll see that they all began with the sun. The sun is a star fueled by nuclear fusion.

The sun is mostly hydrogen. Hydrogen is the simplest atom there is. There is so much of it in the sun that it's being squeezed together. Two hydrogen atoms are fused together, which makes one helium atom. That's what fusion is. When that happens, tremendous energy is released. That's why the sun is hot and bright.

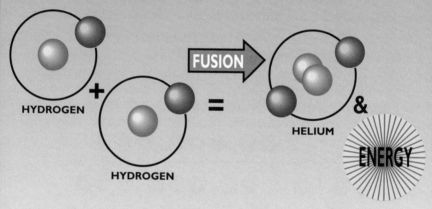

HYDROGEN + HYDROGEN = FUSION HELIUM & ENERGY

Here's the Part Where It Gets Heavy

In about 6 billion years, most of the hydrogen will be gone and the sun will expand. It will eventually touch and destroy all the inner planets – Earth, too. The expansion will take millions of years. Six billion years is more time than you think. The Earth is only 4 1/2 billion years old now.

Not only is life precious, it is also a lot of fun. That means it's worth protecting. We can't do anything to stop the sun from running out of hydrogen. We *can* make sure we protect life on Earth while we are alive on Earth.

Dear Beakman,

How does yeast make bread rise?

Kevin

Dear Kevin,

Men and women have been baking leavened bread for thousands of years. Leavened bread is the kind with bubbles it in. It wasn't until 1876 that Louis Pasteur discovered that the stuff that made bread rise was actually alive.

That stuff is yeast – a microscopic plant. Yeast is a fungus that feeds on sugars. It produces 2 things; alcohol and the gas carbon dioxide.

Cooking destroys the alcohol and kills the yeast. But the bubbles are left behind and that's why bread is soft.

Beakman

Beakman

Growing Yeast

WHAT YOU NEED: 1/4 cup warm (not hot) water - packet of dry yeast - pinch of sugar

WHAT TO DO: Put the sugar into the cup and stir it up. Now sprinkle on the yeast. Don't mix it. Wait 20-30 minutes without looking. What happened?

WHAT IS GOING ON: When you got the yeast wet, you woke it up and it started eating the sugar in the water. Then it grew. Yeast grows 2 different ways. A single cell can divide, or split in 2 pieces. Or it can sprout a bud. Each plant has only one cell. But they grew enough to double or triple in size in your cup. It looks kind of like a monster movie special effect – all gross and slimy. Yeast growing makes carbon dioxide and alcohol.

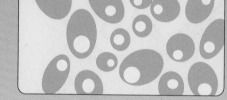

A yeast cell *budding.*

Look at all the bubbles in bread. Yeast makes the gas that blows them up.

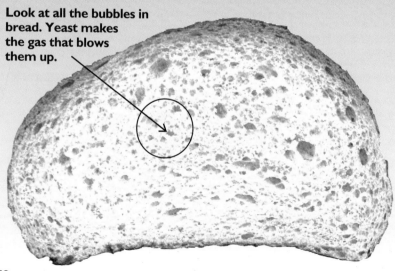

Homemade Bread

Biology and Chemistry in Action

WHAT YOU NEED: The blob of yeast from Experiment #1 - flour - honey - milk - salt - butter - bowls - loaf pans - help from an understanding member of your family

WHAT TO DO: Bring 2 cups of milk to a boil then turn it off and add half a stick of butter cut up into pieces. Let it melt.

Add 2 teaspoons salt and 2 tablespoons honey. Mix it all up and let it cool. If it's hot, you'll kill your yeast. When your milk-mix is cooled off and just warm, dump in the yeast glop and stir. Now add 3 cups flour and mix it all really well. Add another 3 cups flour. This part will be hard to stir. When it's one big clump, dump it out onto a table sprinkled with flour. Punch it, fold it, moosh, mash, and smash it. This is called kneading.

Kneading makes a chemical called gluten. Gluten is the wall of the bubbles. The more you knead the better. Do it for 15 minutes. It feels really good to knead bread. And it is a terrific thing to do if you feel a little down in the dumps. It makes you feel better.

Put the dough into a bowl, cover it with a towel and do something else for an hour and a half. Then dump it out again. It'll be a lot bigger from all the gas the yeast made. Smash it again for a couple of minutes; cut it in 2; put it into 2 greased loaf pans; cover them and leave them alone for 45 minutes. It gives the yeast more time to grow. Now bake the bread at 400° for 30 minutes. When the bread is cool, slice and eat it. You will be amazed at the taste!

When your bread cooked, the alcohol evaporated. But that doesn't happen at a brewery. There, yeast feeds on soaked grains and turns them into beer. Also, the carbon dioxide from yeast gives beer its fizz.

I really don't have all the answers to the questions you guys send into my comic strip. But I do learn more every week – with your help. You guys have great questions. And I want to know what the answers are. So I go to the library and find out. Libraries are our treasure houses of ideas, information and opinions.

Anyone can do the same thing. The only thing is, you need a question that's really important to you. You can't fake it. If you really don't care about the answer, you won't be able to dig through the library and find out. Remember that a question is a very powerful thing. Keep asking them.

Beakman

Free Information

Free libraries are a pretty new idea. They started as a political movement in the late 1800s. The idea was that people needed free and uncensored access to all information so that they could make up their own minds about stuff. The goal of the movement was better democracy. People involved in it said we need to be informed to make good decisions.

In 1898, a very rich guy, named Andrew Carnegie joined the movement and gave it lots of money. He built 2,509 libraries all over the United States and Canada. It cost him millions of dollars. He gave cities the libraries if they promised to keep them free and not censor them. (Censor means that someone else decides what you can and you cannot find out about.)

The guy who figured out how to number the books in the library was a little strange. His name was Melvil Dewey and for fun he wouldn't play. Instead he would alphabetize the things in his mother's kitchen and the canned food.

Figuring Things Out
A Procedure

STEP 1: First, you have to have a question. It has to be your own question because then you'll really care about the answer. These are just sample questions:

- How tall was a Tyrannosaurus Rex?
- How do ballet dancers stay up on their toes like that?
- What is the deal with a curve ball?
- How can you fold paper into a flying bird?

You need to have one that you care about. The neat thing about a library is that *You Can* ask any question in the world. So think about it.

STEP 2: Go to the library. This will be easier than you think. Ask a parent to take you there. Usually one will. People actually like the idea of the library a lot.

You may have to wait until there is time. But *You Can* get someone to take you if you keep asking and are patient. When you go, take a pencil and paper.

STEP 3: There are four ways to find stuff in the library:

- By the subject of your question
- By the title of a book, tape or film
- By the name of the writer
- Ask a librarian

The last one is the one librarians like the most. They're very turned-on people and helping you is fun for them because they get to find out your answers, too.

You Can look up books, tapes and magazines by their (1) title, by (2) the name of their author or by (3) their subject.

STEP 4: Here are the numbers for the books that answer the sample questions.

- Dinosaur books have the number 568
- Ballet books are 792.8
- Baseball books are 796
- Books on paper folding (origami) are 745.54

Borrow the books or tapes and take them home for free!